I0112615

"*Clean Winners* demonstrates how many companies have lost their way by isolating sustainability goals from business value. When combined with customer needs and innovation, sustainability becomes a powerful differentiator."

—**FLORENT MENEGAUX**, CEO, Michelin

"*Clean Winners* sets an inspiring and practical path for businesses to transform their sustainability strategies by reshaping the economy and ecosystems and bringing together sustainability and progress."

—**JEAN-PASCAL TRICOIRE**, Chairman, Schneider Electric

"Goutam Challagalla and Frédéric Dalsace present a compelling and modern framework centered on the concept of resonance—the idea that sustainability, when authentically embedded in a company's value proposition, can amplify customer value and drive competitive advantage. *Clean Winners* offers a customer-oriented perspective that aligns with the future of business: one where value creation and sustainability are mutually reinforcing. A must-read for executives seeking to leverage sustainability to increase customer value."

—**GUILHERME LOUREIRO**, Regional CEO, Walmart Canada, Chile, Central America, and Mexico; coauthor, *Reinventing the Leader*

"Goutam Challagalla and Frédéric Dalsace make sustainability resonate—turning it into something every customer wants to buy. Thus sustainability moves to the heart of business operations and strategy, and whether customers care about it or not, sustainable products will be bought, and, in the end, both customers and the planet win."

—**JØRGEN VIG KNUDSTORP**, former chairman and CEO, the Lego Group; member of the board, Nike and Starbucks

"*Clean Winners* offers readers a clear new path on how to win in sustainability's next phase. Goutam Challagalla and Frédéric Dalsace provide groundbreaking insights into a tool to innovate for better products and services, creating true value for consumers."

—**HIROSHI IGARASHI,** President and Global CEO, Dentsu

"*Clean Winners* is a must-read for every CEO and executive who is tired of sustainability being treated as a cost center. It proves that, when done right, sustainability drives innovation, efficiency, growth, and profit. A powerful way to reframe our thinking and engage businesses on a new path to value creation while still delivering on sustainability challenges."

—**LOÏC MOUTAULT,** Global President, Mars Petcare

"Goutam Challagalla and Frédéric Dalsace offer an insightful rethink of sustainability in business. They challenge conventional wisdom and present actionable strategies to drive customer value, product innovation, and business growth. Sharp, practical, and thought-provoking. *Clean Winners* asks us to put customer value at the heart of sustainable business."

—**ADOLFO ORIVE,** President and CEO, Tetra Pak

"*Clean Winners* shows how the ability of business to solve society's sustainability challenges is clearly linked to high performance. By meeting customer needs we can transform the future."

—**VAGNER REGNO,** President and CEO, Atlas Copco Group

CLEAN WINNERS

GOUTAM CHALLAGALLA
AND FRÉDÉRIC DALSACE

CLEAN WINNERS

★★★★★

SUSTAINABILITY STRATEGY THAT PUTS CUSTOMERS FIRST

HARVARD BUSINESS REVIEW PRESS
BOSTON, MASSACHUSETTS

Printed in the United States of America

10 9 8 7 6 5 4 3 2 1

Cataloging-in-Publication data is forthcoming.

ISBN: 979-8-89279-166-3
eISBN: 979-8-89279-167-0

The paper used in this publication meets the requirements of the American National Standard for Permanence of Paper for Publications and Documents in Libraries and Archives Z39.48-1992.

To my father, who gave me an appreciation for education; to my wife, whose endless support sustains me; and to my daughter, who teaches me to truly live.

—Goutam

To my father, Jean-Pierre Dalsace, and my grandfather, Pierre Dalsace—the "Resonators" in my life.

—Frédéric

CONTENTS

PART THREE
THE ENABLERS

INTRODUCTION

Unsustainable Sustainability

Good Intentions Are Failing to Deliver

Emily is an early sustainability believer; after her college degree in the United States, she completed a master's in sustainability and technology in Switzerland. Among all other firms, she joined Unilever, inspired by its "Sustainable Living Plan" and Paul Polman's vision of "thriving by giving more than we take."

Now with five years into a job where sustainability had been front and center, she was listening to Unilever's new CEO, Heinz Schumacher, announcing how sustainability projects would be scaled back.

"All this for this," she thought . . .

In 2010, the consumer-products giant Unilever was on a roll. More than two billion people in 180 countries were using its trusted products—brands like Lipton, Omo, Dove, and Hellmann's. The firm had its best volume growth for more than thirty years and its new CEO, Paul Polman, charted a course that would soon establish the company as the gold standard for sustainable business. Under the blueprint of the Sustainable Living Plan, Polman publicly committed Unilever to a set of astonishing social, environmental, and business goals. The firm aimed to double its sales. Meanwhile, it promised to halve the environmental footprint of its products, as well as improve the health and well-being of more than a billion people—all within a decade.[1]

In the years that followed, Unilever made good headway. Though its revenue growth through the decade was modest, by the end of 2019 the company's share price had nearly doubled.[2] It had also won a slew of prestigious environmental awards, including being crowned the number one corporate sustainability leader in the Sustainability Leaders survey for the ninth year running.[3]

But then things took a turn for the worse. In the ensuing years, the company's returns lurched through peaks and valleys as they trended precipitously down. From the fall of 2019 to the start of 2024, Unilever's share price staggered along and only after a major strategic course correction under a new CEO, which included massive layoffs, has it begun to pull out of an enduring trough to land virtually where it began five years before.

What happened to Polman's shining vision, the notion that if a business embraces sustainability and social purpose, customers and profits will follow? This idea has become so deeply ingrained in business thinking that it's almost an article of faith. It's spawned a vast industry of consultants and scores of business books—including some famous bestsellers—that promote the conventional wisdom and trot out cases of exemplar companies whose sustainable offerings seem to be the proof in the pudding.

But, as the experience of Unilever and countless like-minded companies show, it's not so simple. Doing well by doing good doesn't always—or even usually—work as advertised. It's not that it can't, just that companies have been doing it wrong. Too often, sustainability drives are themselves unsustainable. Yet it doesn't have to be this way.

Clean Winners is a book about how to get "doing well by doing good" right. In it, we turn conventional thinking about sustainability on its head and offer companies a new and better way forward.

Our four-year collaboration and this book itself stemmed from our own surprise at the gaps in the current sustainability literature and the widespread frustration we've seen among executives with their firms' approach to sustainability. In studying hundreds of businesses, we've found a mishmash of approaches. Despite decades of well-intentioned effort and billions in investment, most businesses still aren't seeing the payoff, and they are still struggling to effectively use sustainability to create value for customers, financial benefits, and real social and environmental good. Companies need to get this piece right. Otherwise, they'll continue to spin their wheels on sustainability, with little to show for their efforts.

We are writing *Clean Winners* because we believe it can provide this missing piece in the sustainable-strategy playbook, a framework that can help companies accomplish what their current sustainability strategies so often fail to do.

Let's set the stage. Stores are awash in products touting their green credentials and companies' ads and annual reports trumpet their commitment to social responsibility and the environment. And yet, for all their goodwill, hard effort, and dollars spent, most firms' approach to sustainability isn't delivering much in the way of profit or shareholder returns.

Why?

The Hype Train and Its Passengers

To understand this disconnect, you must confront an uncomfortable fact about your customers: Despite the avalanche of surveys, articles, and annual reports asserting that customers have an ever-growing desire for sustainable goods, the picture is murky at best.

Clean Winners win because, at the core, they appreciate the fundamental truth that sustainability is never the primary reason any customer makes a purchase. With any purchase, customers (even the most socially and eco-conscious) are primarily trying to get a specific job done. In the words of the celebrated business scholar Clayton Christensen, people "hire" products to do these jobs. They are a means to an end. What matters, then, is less the product's features themselves, but the benefits that the customer is seeking from these features. Nobody goes to the pharmacist because they want to buy a bottle of molecules; they buy a medicine because they want to get better. They're "hiring" the medicine to do a specific job—to restore their health.

Traditionally, these benefits are of two kinds: functional and emotional. A consumer buys a quality mattress for its functional benefit—a good night's sleep. But he may buy a luxury Swiss watch for its emotional benefit—signaling status.

Only after customers find a product that will help them do that job—and only if sustainability is important to them—will they look for a product that, in addition, is less harmful to the environment or better for society. Think about it this way: If sustainability really was a consumer's primary "job to be done," the most committed people wouldn't buy anything at all. Nobody buys detergent to save the planet—they buy it because they need to clean their clothes. Similarly, no one decides to buy an electric car to prevent climate change. They buy a car because they need transportation; reducing their carbon footprint (for some) is an added benefit.

Two additional quirks of customer behavior confuse things further. First, what people claim about their desire for green or socially responsible products—and their willingness to pay more for them—is often at odds with their actual behavior at the cash register. Second, a given customer's attitude about sustainable products can vary from occasion to occasion and from one product to another. The result is that conclusions based on survey responses—for example, that 70% of consumers are willing to pay up to 10% more for sustainable products—should be taken with a grain of salt.

Let's look at just a tiny fraction of the mountain of research out there. In 2023, Bain surveyed over 23,000 consumers across eleven countries and found that 64% reported "high levels of concern" about sustainability.[4] Capgemini reported that 79% of consumers claim they are changing their buying habits based on sustainability.[5] Moreover, a PWC survey concluded—based on consumers' self-reporting—that eight out of ten consumers are willing to pay more for sustainably produced goods.[6] Meanwhile, McKinsey and NielsenIQ claimed that "consumers care about sustainability—and they're backing it up with their wallets."[7]

Addressing a Deutsche Bank conference in 2019, then-Unilever CEO, Alan Jope, made the point this way: "Two-thirds of consumers around the world say they choose brands because of their stand on social issues, and over 90% of millennials say they would switch brands for one which champions a cause."[8]

It's a feel-good story with some elements of truth, but unfortunately, what consumers say they'll do and what they actually do are often very different. In behavioral surveys, people tend to say what will reflect well on them and reinforce the self-image they aspire to. So of course they *say* they care about sustainability, are changing their buying habits accordingly, and are willing to pay a premium for green goods. After all, who's going to admit that they don't care about the planet? And indeed, in 2020, the consulting firm Kearney found that 70% of consumers said they were willing to pay up to 10% more for sustainable products, 15% would pay up to 30% more, and the remaining 15% would be willing to pay over 30% more.[9]

But consider some of the research looking at what consumers actually do. Two studies among scores of similar ones are representative. Using an auction-based approach, a McKinsey study found that the average price premium people would really pay for three staple products making sustainability claims (yogurt, shampoo, and a t-shirt) was a mere 2.2%.[10] And a study by the European ecommerce leader Zalando, involving 2,500 consumers, revealed that consumers pay a lot less attention to sustainability claims than they say they do.[11] In that study, 60% said transparency about sustainability is important to them, but only 20% actively seek such information as part of the purchasing process;

53% said it is important to buy from brands with ethical labor policies, but only 23% ever investigate policies themselves; and 58% believed they should investigate the materials used in making the products they buy, but just 38% regularly check labels for such information.

Sustainability studies exposing this so-called say/do gap abound. Yet they tend to receive less attention than research that confirms what so many academics, consultants, and companies would like to believe about consumers' better nature. That's unfortunate, because these studies point to a more productive way for companies to think about how they should—and shouldn't—use sustainability to engage their customers. Let's look, for instance, at the less obvious, but equally important takeaway from the studies we just cited: All the people who don't care about sustainability are consumers too (and probably your customers)—the 21% who straight-up say they're not changing their buying habits because of it, or the one out of five who admit that they won't pay extra for sustainable goods.

What this data is really telling us is that it's time we think about sustainable offerings the way we think about any good or service. One of the basic rules of marketing—segmentation—applies here too. As the late marketing scholar Ted Levitt said: "If you're not thinking segments, you're not thinking."[12]

We advise companies with sustainable offerings to think of their customers as falling into one of three groups, according to their attitude toward sustainability. The first group are the Greens, who care a lot and will sacrifice some performance or spend more to have it. The second group are the Blues, who care somewhat and, if they don't need to sacrifice much (or ideally at all) on price and performance, tend to prefer sustainable offerings over alternatives. And the final group are the Grays, who don't care about sustainability and may even view it with skepticism.

Even executives who understand this basic type of segmentation often miss that a customer—whether an individual or a company—may shift back and forth among these consumption postures depending on the offering. They may be a Green consumer in one product category (for example, exclusively purchasing clean energy for home or business), Blue in another (preferring recycled packaging when its available and if there's no cost difference), and Gray in another (avoiding sustainable cleaning products or construction materials on the assumption that they will perform less well than their less sustainable equivalents).

We'll explore customer segmentation further in chapter 2 and you'll find it's useful to keep these customer groups top of mind as you progress through the book.

Unconventional Wisdom

We know that taking aim at sustainable-business orthodoxy is a controversial stance—it flies in the face of the optimistic storytelling that so many companies would like to believe. It also seems at conspicuous odds with the reams of research that apparently point to customers' ever-growing desire for ethical, sustainable goods, and that tie sustainable business to outsized returns.

Part of what follows will be a critical examination of this uncomfortable truth, a dive into the years of research that led to our inescapable conclusion. Most of the book, though, is devoted to the positive lessons we learned from our study, executive teaching, and consulting, thus resulting in a new, more clear-eyed and reality-based model for sustainable business in which doing well by doing good actually works.

Ultimately, we are hopeful, despite our contrarian premise. What most companies have gotten wrong is, in a way, quite simple. They have assumed that most consumers and businesses care enough about supporting the social good and protecting the environment that they'll make compromises or pay a premium for products and services that do that. Churn out sustainable offerings and the profits will surely flow, right? The disappointing truth is that, actually, no, by and large they won't. Faced with a choice between a sustainable product or service and the cheaper alternative that's just as good or better, customers tend to vote with their wallets.

This could be an insurmountable obstacle for sustainability strategy. But in fact, it points to a clear way forward, one that a few companies are already putting to the test. The solution at the heart of our book is for companies to flip their conventional sustainability thinking. Companies need not ask: "How can we make our offerings more sustainable without raising prices or compromising performance?" Instead, companies should ask: "How can we use sustainability to improve the performance of our products, sell them for less, make them cheaper to use, or all of the above?" Sustainability should be a catalyst of innovation that drives customer value.

Viewed through this lens, sustainability becomes an intrinsic, value-generating element of an offering, rather than an add-on with potential costs for both companies and customers. Even those Gray customers who don't care about sustainability will seek out these products simply because they're better than the alternatives.

Look at Electrolux, which shrewdly developed a special drum for its washers that is gentler on clothes during wash cycles, such that the clothes last longer. This saves consumers money (since they don't have to buy new clothes as often) while reducing carbon emissions, waste, and water use. Or consider the Minnesota-based Revier Cattle Company, whose sustainable farming practices produce superior meats that consistently beat competitors in blind taste tests. On the B2B (business-to-business) side, there's John Deere, which has shifted from selling farm equipment to selling farm productivity, using digital technologies to reduce farmers' use of fuel and herbicides, thus lowering their costs, increasing their yields, and simplifying regulatory compliance.

Companies like Electrolux, Revier, and Deere are what we call "Clean Winners." In the chapters that follow, we'll explore how Clean Winners use sustainability to create new customer value and increase profits.

And, just as important, we'll show how businesses can reimagine their sustainability approach and start on the journey to becoming Clean Winners themselves. To do this, they must harness what we call "Resonance": leveraging sustainability to increase customer value—a concept that we explore in detail later in the book. First, it's useful to understand the mindset of Clean Winners—how they think about their customers and sustainability. Table I-1 captures some important distinctions

TABLE I-1

Conventional versus Clean Winners strategy

	Conventional sustainability thinking	**Clean Winners thinking**
Perspective	Normative: "This is how we believe, and want, the world to work"	Factual: "This is how the world actually works"
Perception of customer beliefs	"Most customers will care" (about sustainability)	"Not everybody cares"
Evangelism	If customers don't believe in sustainability, convert them	We are not here to change customers' beliefs
Objectives	Firms need to have an independent sustainability strategy because: • It is a differentiator • It can reduce risk, enhance reputation, and provide continued license to operate	Firms need to integrate sustainability into their strategy because: • Sustainability itself isn't a differentiator that drives purchases. Customer value created by sustainability is. • It can create "reasons to buy" for *every* customer, whether they care about sustainability or not
Success roadmap	Sell customers on the social and environmental benefits of sustainability	Sell customers on price and performance, and communicate sustainability element only to those who care
Messaging and communication	Highlight the sustainability benefit: "We help save water because it is scarce"	Highlight the traditional benefits: "We lower your water bills"
Lasting impact	Conventional sustainability thinking only weakly drives growth and has fragile social and environmental impact	Clean Winners thinking drives growth and creates long-term, "sustainable" social and environmental impact

between conventional sustainability-strategy thinking and how Clean-Winner companies think differently. We will cover these differences in the different book chapters.

Before saying more about Resonance and the book's plan, let's return to Unilever to see how this celebrated company's sustainability strategy led it astray.

The Complicated Case of Unilever

We're based at IMD, a business school in Lausanne, Switzerland, with sweeping views of Lake Geneva to the south framed by the towering French Alps on the opposite shore. Businesses send individuals and teams from all over the world for the school's executive education offerings, among them some of the courses we teach on sustainability strategy. For years, we've featured Unilever in our teaching, and like most observers, we single it out as a best-practice example of a flourishing, ethical, and green business. Our message to executives was clear: "Here is a company that got sustainability right."

But in recent years—as we've studied the company and combed the rich academic literature and consumer and trade press to understand its workings—a more nuanced (and in some ways troubling) picture has emerged. It is a picture that has powerfully informed our thinking about sustainability strategy.

In 2009, it was Paul Polman, the company's new chief executive, who set Unilever on its epic sustainability journey. Polman made radical changes to the way the business operated, none more so than abandoning quarterly reporting of results, which he did on his first day as CEO.[13] He argued that such reporting caused a "three-month rat race" that worked against bigger goals and ideals.

The move opened the door in 2010 for Polman's Unilever Sustainable Living Plan (USLP), a prospectus that committed the firm to the ambitious goals we mentioned earlier—and more.[14] It aimed to help more than a billion people (consumers) take action to improve their health and well-being through a series of measures. These goals were as follows:

- Decouple its growth from its environmental impact—achieving absolute reductions across the product lifecycle.
- Halve the environmental footprint of the making and use of its products.
- Enhance the livelihoods of hundreds of thousands of people in its supply chain.
- Somewhere along the way, double the size of its business.

These were extraordinarily bold commitments. Unilever made these changes because they were driven by presumed customer preferences: "Consumers around the world want reassurance that the products they buy are ethically sourced and protect Earth's natural resources," the USLP says. The mantra applied equally to Unilever's B2B market as to its B2C (business-to-consumer): "Many retailers have sustainability goals of their own," the SLP said. "They need the support of suppliers like Unilever if they are to achieve them."[15]

The key message—and Polman's guiding principle—was that a company and brands with a sustainability angle would drive growth. Businesses and consumers were demanding sustainability benefits from the products they purchased, company executives came to believe, and therefore those companies that were committed to delivering them would thrive. Early evidence supported the claim. Unilever recorded strong results in the years following the launch of its USLP. In 2018, it reported that its most sustainable brands grew 69% faster than the rest of the business.[16] In 2020, Standard & Poor's Dow Jones Sustainability Index named it the global leader in the sustainability of personal products.[17] In 2021, it was crowned for the eleventh time as the number one corporate sustainability leader in the Sustainability Leaders Survey.[18] And in 2022, it was given the Renewable Energy 100 Market Trailblazer Award at Climate Week NYC.[19]

Yet despite these achievements, Polman was thinking bigger still. His 2021 book, *Net Positive: How Companies Thrive by Giving More Than They Take*, is a manifesto for a form of capitalism still alien to most companies, customers, and investors. It argues that firms should take responsibility for all the impacts they cause—whether intended or unintended, direct or indirect—via their global supply chains.

Net Positive advocates that firms act in the mutual best interests of *all* their stakeholders, and that generating shareholder value is a result of this approach, rather than its primary goal. It urges companies not to avoid persistent critics, such as Greenpeace and Oxfam, but to actively embrace them, partnering with them to improve practice. It is companies' own duty, *Net Positive* says, to liaise with lawmakers to improve regulatory frameworks so firms can meet sustainability goals.

It looked to casual observers like the company had cracked the code—that Unilever was leading a global charge that could transform how all of business approached sustainability. Polman left in 2018 and Unilever's share price rose to record highs under the leadership of the new CEO, Alan Jope, but the rally was short-lived. As we mentioned, in the ensuing years, the company's returns ricochetted around, but ultimately headed down; from the fall of 2019 to the start of 2025, Unilever's share price fluctuated continuously.[20] As we go to press, despite the uptick under Jope, the company's share price is lagging its 2020 high.

Investors, naturally, were spooked by the company's struggles. It was Terry Smith who lowered the boom. Smith, chief executive of London-based Fundsmith, an investment firm managing £36 billion in assets, singled out Unilever's sustainability focus as a dangerous distraction.

Smith has a signature style and while his quoted statements might seem vaguely amusing or sarcastic, they carry an important warning.

"A company which feels it has to define the purpose of Hellmann's mayonnaise has in our view clearly lost the plot. The Hellmann's brand has existed since 1913, so we would guess that by now consumers have figured out its purpose: spoiler alert—salads and sandwiches."[21]

Smith's repeated accusations that Unilever was prioritizing sustainability pronouncements over creating commercial value prefaced more bad news. In July 2024, the company announced that it would cut one third of its European office jobs. This would eliminate about 3,200 jobs. These reductions would be on top of 7,500 jobs that were to be slashed globally.[22]

Smith's critique may have been abrasive and simplistic, but our research suggests it's not entirely off base. It appears to us that Unilever's single-minded focus on sustainability—what we call its mindset—contributed substantially to it sputtering performance.

Unilever fell into the trap of chasing too many sustainability targets and failing to create new value for its customers as it pursued its unwavering course. The company's new CEO, Hein Schumacher, who took the reins in the summer of 2023, has abandoned the USLP. He is clear that the presumed relationship between sustainability (doing a lot of good) and shareholder value (doing well) has not panned out. He was reported as telling investors that the company's sustainability goals were too "aspirational" and that "our efforts are being spread too thinly." He added: "We have too many long-term commitments that failed to make sufficient short-term impact, and the latter is what the world really needs right now."[23]

The company's goals to become net zero across Scope 1, 2 and 3 emissions by 2039, halve the footprint of its products, and create a one-billion-euro climate and nature fund to support that effort have been revised.[24] Now, Unilever will focus its sustainability efforts in four areas—climate, nature, plastic waste, and livelihoods. It will no longer set company-wide goals but will instead let division heads and brand owners determine the right metrics.[25]

Obviously, there's no single reason why Unilever struggled in the latter part of Polman's tenure. One likely contributor is that prioritizing sustainability across its portfolio distracted managers from the focus on product-strategy fundamentals. At the same time, consumers' growing cost-consciousness surely contributed to the pressures on the company's performance. In short, the company's sometimes pricey sustainable brands (think Ben & Jerry's) were having trouble competing with cheaper private labels and other more affordable alternatives in a world where many—we'd argue most—consumers prioritize price over sustainability.

The Truth About the "Business Case for Sustainability"

Let's start by acknowledging that sometimes you can in fact draw a clear line connecting sustainability and profits. The famously green and socially conscious outdoor apparel company Patagonia is a case in point. With its sustainable manufacturing, circular business model, celebrated conservation efforts, and sustainability-forward marketing, it's a gold-standard eco-friendly firm. It also generates an estimated $100 million in profits year after year.[26] But it's only able to do this because it can charge its affluent, eco-conscious customers heart-stopping prices for its very green, high-quality products (for example, its Stormshadow parka retails for $899). For this rarified customer segment, the brand's green credentials coupled with superior quality and robust guarantees sustains its high prices and feeds Patagonia's profits. Other examples also come to mind—Whole Foods, whose similarly affluent and environmentally minded customers don't flinch at paying nearly $30 a pound for its super-fresh, sustainably sourced sea bass; and Tesla, whose high-performance, zero-emissions electric cars start at around $40,000 for the entry-level Model 3 and can approach $100,000 for the top-of-the-line Model X Plaid.

But these familiar cases are outliers, sustainable brands whose profits hinge on having an upscale, relatively price-insensitive customer base. In general, though, the evidence linking sustainability and profits is a lot weaker, or certainly more qualified, than the sometimes-overheated reporting suggests. On average, companies' return on sustainable products remains modest at best and realized only over the long term. And the supposedly strong connection between sustainability and solid shareholder returns is far from clear-cut.

Then what *can* we say with confidence about the business case for sustainability? Researchers have been studying this for decades, generating literally thousands of studies. Most of the studies do show a small but positive relationship between a firm's sustainability actions and financial performance. As of July 2024, we found 230 academic review articles summarizing prior research, including more than two dozen meta-analyses. One 2018 study, a so-called second order meta-analysis of twenty-five previous meta-analyses yielding one million observations, came to an unambiguous conclusion: "The business case for being a good firm is undeniable."[27]

Undeniable, yes, but weak. The giant 2018 study with its million observations concluded that the weighted average correlation between doing good and doing well is only about 0.12—statistically significant for academic researchers yet very small in the real world. Of course, an average is just that; some companies are struggling or even failing to demonstrate a viable sustainability strategy. A few are hitting it out of the park.

As the thousands of studies on the topic attest, understanding what accounts for the connection between doing good and doing well is difficult. There are a plethora of confounding factors complicating the research and its conclusions: How do you define "sustainability"? How do you measure "doing good"? How do you capture and account for impacts that may take years to materialize? And how can you reliably attribute a specific business outcome to a specific sustainability initiative so as to nail down cause and effect? Could it be that firms that do well invest in doing good, rather than the other way around? And, if your new fair-trade product with sustainable packaging and eco-friendly ingredients turns a profit, how do you know which—or if—any of these accounts for the margin?

The dubious case of cause and effect

It's human nature to see two things happening in sequence and assume the first one causes the second. In our executive education classes, we have a favorite chart to make this point—a graph showing country-by-country per capita measures of chocolate consumption on the one hand and the concentration of Nobel Laureates in the population on the other. The correlation is massive (>.90). Clearly, eating more chocolate will increase your chances of winning a Nobel Prize!

Unilever's 2018 report stated that its most sustainable brands grew 69% faster than the rest of the business.[28] McKinsey and NielsenIQ concluded that the more sustainability-related claims a product made, the faster it grows.[29]

It's possible they're observing true causes and effects, but alternative explanations readily come to mind. For example, could the method Unilever used account for the observed effect? How were the brands selected? Most likely, this was not a random process, and its leading brands were considered first. Couldn't this have had an influence? Did the communication budget that these brands spent to make their purpose known increase a lot? If so, is it fair to compare these heavily promoted brands with regularly promoted brands?

Or take the McKinsey/NielsenIQ study's conclusion that adding four or more claims—things like "all natural," and "cage-free"—increases sales. It's likely that any time a product adds so many new claims, it's undergone a repositioning accompanied by a substantial marketing effort. For example, Unilever's Dove "Real Beauty" campaign added a sustainability claim (female empowerment) to a product, accompanied by a major marketing push. Under these conditions, it's not surprising that such products would show stronger growth. So is it fair to attribute this growth to actual improvements in the products' sustainability?

Again, we're not disputing that sustainability can have a positive impact on sales—we believe that it clearly can. It's just that any company's assertion that its products' sustainability *caused* dramatic growth should be carefully evaluated, and alternative explanations considered. Unfortunately, too many firms skip this sort of careful study because they lack the resources to look closely, or they have a sustainability mindset that discourages any challenge to its agenda. The result can be a lot of well-intentioned but often costly and poorly focused (or even wasted) effort.

How sustainability really drives performance

In the select cases when sustainability clearly *does* boost performance, how does that work? The answer to this question can provide the guidance companies need to soundly steer their sustainability investments; indeed, it reveals the rationale underlying the successful strategies of companies that practice and achieve Resonance.

Figure I-1 presents a simplified model, based on our own research and research done by others, that captures the generally accepted understanding of the ways sustainability can lead to profits. The model distinguishes between direct drivers such as cutting costs and increasing sales, and four principal indirect drivers: speeding up innovation, transforming the company's sense of purpose and motivating employees, enhancing reputation and building social capital, and reducing risks.[30]

Each of the indirect direct drivers has the potential to boost financial performance, but it's innovation, at the bottom left, that is the

FIGURE I-1

Disentangling the business case of sustainability

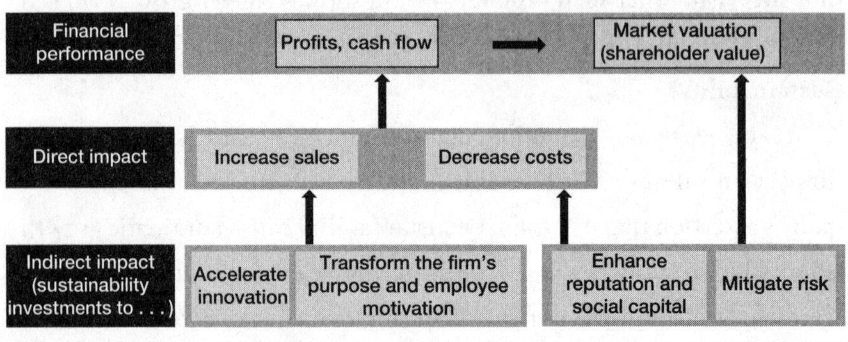

primary focus. Obviously, using sustainability to enhance employee motivation, improve reputation, and mitigate risk can contribute to a company's performance. But our research suggests that only disciplined attention to sustainability *innovations* that create value for customers, and embedding this approach into the company's overall strategy, will cause a consistent improvement in overall performance. This is Resonance. It explains why, while companies *in aggregate* see little effect of sustainability on profits and returns, a select, innovative few are seeing a dramatic impact. It's these customer-focused "Resonators" that we believe will win the sustainability race and become Clean Winners.

As the following chapters will show, Resonators do more than just create innovative offerings for sustainability-minded customers; they also provide compelling reasons for *all* customers to choose their products, even those who don't care about sustainability. For these customers, better performance or affordability is a reason to buy; for the more socially and environmentally conscious customers, price and performance is also a reason to buy, but the sustainability element provides additional value.

"Navigating the world as it is" vs. "hoping to change the world"

Academic research has provided a foundation, legitimizing the idea that, under certain circumstances, sustainability efforts can enhance financial performance. Meanwhile, many stakeholders in sustainability, each with their own agendas, have embraced this notion without fully considering its limitations (or sometimes, conspicuously ignoring them). They let ethical concerns confuse the business rationale, exhorted firms to keep doing what they were doing, and even accelerated this work, all because they believed it was the right thing to do. And, when companies began to find that their sustainability efforts weren't paying off as expected, the frequent explanation offered was that they were simply ahead of their time and that customers will eventually come around on their own, or if not, they should be persuaded to put sustainability first.

Resonator companies view the world as it is, rather than how it should be or how they want it to be. They are not out to make customers change, and they are not waiting for customers to change on their own. Instead, they're meeting their customers where they are today, and using sustainability to do it. It's not rocket science. It's basic customer-centricity—putting customer value first.

Returning to Unilever, the company's new CEO, Hein Schumacher, is now leading a major course correction that we believe signals it's on track to become a Resonator—and eventually, a Clean Winner.

"In recent years," Schumacher has acknowledged, "the debate around brands, sustainability and purpose has arguably generated more heat than light. The topics have been conflated, and the business case has got confused. . . . We will not force fit purpose across our entire [brand] portfolio. For some brands, it simply won't be relevant, and that's OK."[31]

He has not stopped there, making one more crucial shift that is reorienting the company toward delivering "unmissable product superiority"—in other words, customer value.

But what about sustainability? "By increasing the other key attributes alongside product and price," Schumacher said, "we can give proper weight to increasingly important determinants, like desirable packaging, and sustainability, which is key now for many consumers."[32] We wish Schumacher had been more specific on the role of sustainability, something along the lines of: "We will use sustainability as a key driver of product performance and affordability." But we believe that's the direction Schumaker is guiding the company. Case in point: In a commercial for Unilever's new Persil Wonder Wash detergent, the world-renowned sprinter Usain Bolt announces, "Fast just got better," while pitching the innovative formulation's ability to wash clothes in just fifteen minutes. "Sustainability" isn't mentioned in the ad—the point is that the product solves a customer's issue better than the competition and, incidentally, cleans so fast that it saves water and electricity.

By taking such a practical, no-nonsense approach to sustainability, companies and products like these will help ensure that sustainable business goes decisively mainstream, becoming the default approach to creating competitive goods and services. In the long run, we believe this approach will mean that, of all businesses, Clean Winners stand to make the most significant impact on sustainability.

How We've Organized the Book

Chapter 1 is an important preamble. We explore how companies fall into four groups based on the customer value they create through their sustainability investments and the impacts these investments have. Understanding these four approaches will help you determine where your company falls and how, as you'll learn in the chapters to come, you can evolve your current strategy to a more competitive and value-creating approach.

Clean Winners is then divided into two parts. Part One introduces the Resonator model, as well as three interrelated sustainability pathways, each of which gets its own chapter.

Chapter 2 explains the concept of Resonance, the path chosen by Clean Winners. We show how it is fundamentally different from the other three approaches. You will see how resonant companies question five "common beliefs" about sustainability in order to reexamine the link with customer value creation. This chapter also provides a model that we will use throughout the book, and delineates the three resonance pathways. You will see how we take a holistic approach, linking customer value, business inefficiencies, and sustainability externalities.

In chapter 3, we explore the first resonance pathway, Product Resonance. This chapter shows how resonance approaches can improve the value of companies' products and services.

Chapter 4 describes the second pathway, Usage Resonance. This shows how Resonance can be introduced into business models to optimize *utilization* of firms' products and services. By helping customers use a product more efficiently—either by reducing misuse, limiting underuse, or promoting reuse—companies can profitably enhance both sustainability and customer value.

Chapter 5 examines the third pathway, Strategic Resonance. This is derived from finding adjacencies. In this strategy, companies profitably move into adjacent markets in ways that provide enhanced traditional benefits for customers already in those markets, while delivering sustainability payoffs as well.

Part Two of the book digs into how companies can put these strategies to use, examining three essential pillars of strategy execution: digital capability, targeted communications, and adaptive leadership. Through these three enablers, resonant firms can evolve into Clean Winners.

In chapter 6, we delve first into how integrator companies use digital technologies to enhance the customer value and sustainability impact of existing products and services, or to create altogether new ones. We also explore how these companies are using digital to extend the reach of their resonant offerings and to generate data that can increase the value they deliver.

We then look, in chapter 7, at how Resonator companies leverage different communication practices to advance their sustainability strategies. Unlike other firms, they develop a contingent strategy to decide whether to communicate on sustainability benefits at the product level. At the corporate level, they don't seek to highlight initiatives, progress, or purpose, but rather integrate sustainability with the firm's overall strategy.

We conclude with a chapter on leadership that weaves it all together and issues a call to arms. Few companies are full Resonators; some do only what they need to stay ahead of regulations; others are opportunists, jumping on the sustainability bandwagon only when they see immediate gains to be had; and others put sustainability at the heart of everything they do, even if it compromises customer value or profitability.

We explain how leaders of each company type can begin shifting strategy toward the Resonance model. For those that are already Resonators, the book provides clarity and guidance for continuing on the path—and evolving into a new generation of Clean Winners.

Let's get started.

PART ONE

THE FUNDAMENTALS

1

The Four Mindsets

Aiming for Resonance

Oliver grew frustrated during the Executive Committee meeting as Ella, the Chief Sustainability Officer, proposed expensive sustainability projects that weren't required by law. Earlier, his own R&D budget had faced intense financial scrutiny, yet these initiatives faced no questions. Everybody was nodding.

He asked, "So, Ella, what financial return can we expect from these sustainability projects?" She replied, "That's a tough question in our field, but they will undoubtedly enhance our firm's reputation." Oliver pressed, "Will we recoup our investments?" She responded, "Research suggests that 'doing well by doing good' works, and ultimately, we believe it's the right thing to do."

Is Ella right? It seems that in the past this type of thinking was routinely accepted: Sustainability was getting special treatment. But should it? Resonators think otherwise; they stand behind Oliver.

We have looked at many firms' sustainability strategy in our research. At first, it looks like companies fall into just one of two big sustainability buckets: Those that live and breathe social purpose and being Green—eco-friendly firms like Unilever, Whole Foods, and

Burt's Bees—and everyone else. Of course, it's not so simple. Like customers, companies fall on a spectrum from Green to Gray. For some, sustainability is their guiding light. Social and environmental stewardship come first in everything they do. For others, sustainability, to the extent they engage at all, is a matter of compliance—doing the least they need to do to stay in business. And then there's most companies—the legions of businesses large and small—that fall somewhere in between.

Where does your company stand? Or, as we like to put it, what is your company's sustainability "mindset?" What does everyone from leadership down to the rank and file *think* about sustainability, and how does this translate into action?

Let's examine the four fundamental sustainability mindsets we've uncovered and show you how to determine which one best describes your firm. Having a clear understanding of your firm's mindset is an essential first step for any company that hopes to become a Clean Winner.

Mind Your Mindset

We have studied the sustainability strategies and investments of hundreds of companies and talked with countless executives about their firms' approaches. At first, the differences in their approaches seemed as great as their similarities; some prioritized reducing the carbon footprint, some focused on green ingredients in their products, some put social equity first. Some companies did all these things, while others did only what was needed to meet local regulations. But, as our research grew, a useful way of sorting these firms came into focus: grouping companies according to the degree of their sustainability investments on the one hand, and the scope of their initiatives on the other. This way of sorting companies lends itself to a simple 2×2 that captures four

FIGURE 1-1

The four sustainability mindsets

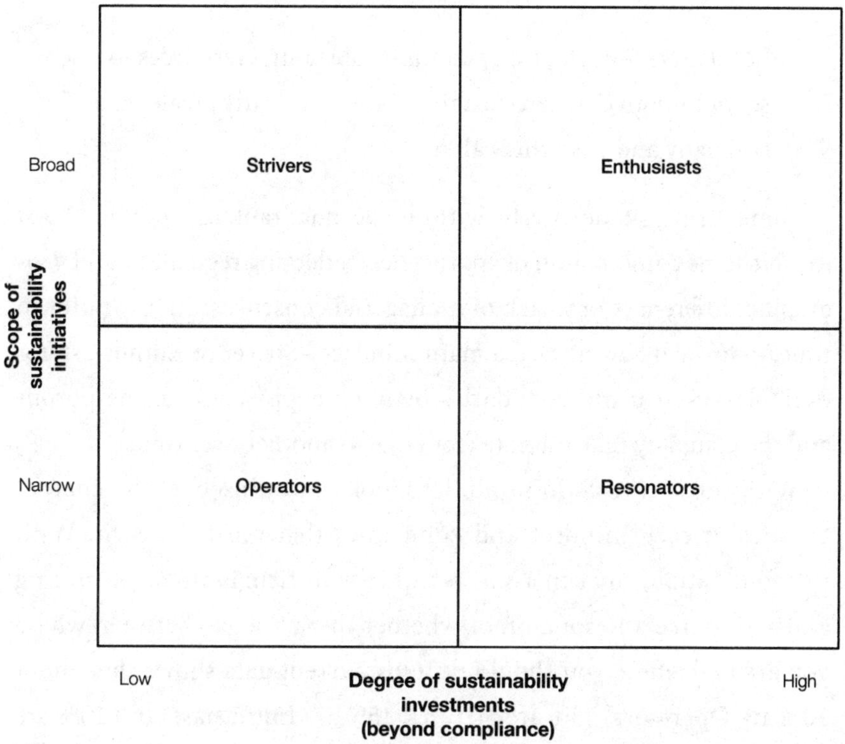

Scope of sustainability initiatives	Low	High
Broad	Strivers	Enthusiasts
Narrow	Operators	Resonators

Degree of sustainability investments (beyond compliance): Low → High

broad mindsets, which we've labeled Operators, Strivers, Enthusiasts, and Resonators (see figure 1-1).

We'll do a deep dive on each of these, but by way of introduction here is the top-line take:

- **Operators**—invest conservatively in a few, select initiatives, doing the minimum needed to comply with rules and keep their license to operate.
- **Strivers**—likewise limit their investments, but spread them opportunistically across projects they think will generate quick profits and enhance social capital.

- **Enthusiasts**—put sustainability at the heart of everything they do, investing heavily across a profusion of activities, expecting that long-term growth and profits will follow.
- **Resonators**—strategically commit substantial resources to a select set of initiatives where sustainability will clearly create value for company and customers alike.

Some firms sit decisively within one quadrant or another. Most exhibit some combination of approaches, reflecting regulatory and geographic differences or a lack of managerial consensus. At any point in time, firms will hew toward a main mindset—Striver or Enthusiast, for example—even if the boundaries between approaches can be porous and the company may migrate from one to another over time.

With those caveats in mind, let's look more closely at the characteristics of each mindset and companies that illustrate each. With this foundation, you can assess whether your firm is already thinking and acting like a Resonator, or whether there is a gap between where you are and where you should be. Our current data shows that about 30% are Operators, 45% are Strivers, 15% are Enthusiast, and 10% are Resonators. While we have found these percentages to be relatively stable the past few years, shifting regulations or geopolitical realities can make a difference. Our hope is that more firms become Resonators over time.

Sustainability Operators

Operators have one dominant sustainability goal: retaining their social, legal, and customer license to operate. Their focus is primarily on risk mitigation and compliance, and they will engage in the few sustainability initiatives required to satisfy regulators, employees, customers, investors, or other stakeholders.

We'd like to introduce a useful nuance here regarding sustainability investments. Bernard Meunier, EVP at Nestlé, brought this to our attention. "Right to Play" investments are those that keep a firm in the game. "Right to Stay" investments are forward-looking sustainability investments to improve the resiliency of a business. Kit Kat's global head, Chris O'Donnell, spoke to us about their Income Accelerator Program that aimed to improve the livelihoods of cocoa farmers. These investments are necessary to ensure Kit Kat has an adequate supply of cocoa, whose prices hit a forty-seven-year high in 2025. "Right to Win" investments are genuinely optional investments made by firms that believe they can win through sustainability.

The key focus of Operators is Right to Play investments. But given the pressures on business to embrace sustainability and tout their good deeds, Operators are often reluctant to acknowledge their defensive posture toward social and environmental commitments. But there are plenty of Operators out there; about 30% of those we've studied would qualify as Operators. This finding aligns with the conclusion of a recent IBM study, involving 5,000 C-level executives across twenty-two industries and twenty-two countries, that spending on sustainability reporting exceeded spending on sustainability innovation by 43%.[1]

Why this mindset?

Given the potential for sustainability to do more for a firm than simply keeping it out of trouble, why do so many companies assume the Operators' defensive stance? In our research and conversations with executives within these companies, a few common threads emerged.

Many think sustainability advocates have exaggerated its importance to customers, particularly with respect to climate. There's an element of truth to this. Even Green-leaning customers may only be Green some of the time, and a significant customer segment is simply Gray—largely indifferent about brands' sustainability posture.

For some Operators, a decision to do just the minimum required lies in skepticism about environmental science generally and the belief that climate science remains inconclusive. These companies bristle at and even lobby against environmental regulations that increase the cost of their operations and that they feel are rooted in dubious science and unfairly disadvantage them.

Even those Operator firms that accept the need for sustainability regulation tend to experience compliance as a costly burden and sustainability broadly as an impediment to new growth. A CSO of a large global firm mentioned to us that her company had to deal with 18,000 changes to sustainability regulations in 2024 alone. Another large company CEO told us that he has sixty full-time employees whose job is to ensure that the firm simply meets regulatory requirements. A CSO at another firm complained that she spends 90% of her time ensuring compliance and feels she has no choice but to just make Right to Play investments. And an executive at another large firm said she expects the company to spend up to $60 million in the coming years just to comply with the EU's Corporate Sustainability Reporting Directive (CSRD).

Emerging-economy Operators face an added compliance concern in their dealings with developed-country markets. Regulations in these markets often focus on the "E" (environment) in ESG (that is, environmental, social, and governance), when the "S"—social initiatives—are, by far, emerging-economy businesses' biggest priority. They worry that the cost of being compliant is making it hard for them to do the things that are most immediately important for their own society. Airlangga Hartarto, Indonesia's economic affairs minister, for example, echoed the sentiment of many business leaders from his region when he called the EU's law restricting trade of goods from deforested land as "regulatory imperialism" that hurts small farmers.[2]

Given Operators' experience and perceptions, it should be little surprise that their spending on sustainability initiatives is largely limited to compliance. But how does this narrow focus affect customer value?

Impact on Customer Value

As we saw in figure 1-1, Operators make relatively small optional investments across just a few initiatives. The value those investments create is plotted in figure 1-2.

Each dot represents a sustainability initiative, which can range from product R&D to process improvements to corporate social responsibility (CSR) activities, and the x-axis shows the size of the investment. The size of the dot represents the sustainability impact: A large dot would indicate a larger expected impact. The scope of sustainability initiatives is captured by the number of dots—the more there are, the broader the scope. The y-axis shows the customer value created by each initiative, as gauged by its affordability and how customers judge its performance. Think of "performance" in a broad way—product benefits such as quality,

FIGURE 1-2

Operator mindset and customer value

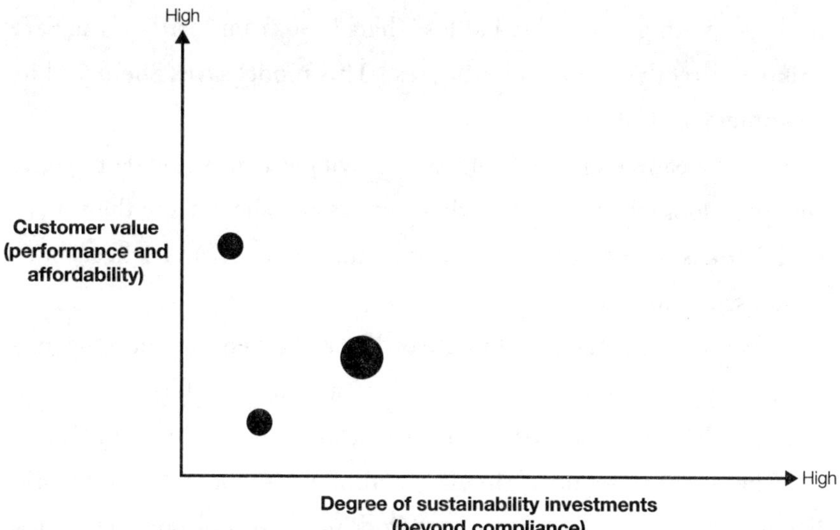

Note: Each black dot is a sustainability initiative (e.g., product R&D, process improvements, corporate social responsibility). More dots indicate more initiatives (or scope).

reliability, durability, improved customer experience, lower cost, faster delivery, and so on, all the attributes that driver customer purchases. The resulting picture should be no surprise: Operators' narrow approach to sustainability creates little new customer value. It's a missed opportunity.

The Singapore-based fast-fashion company, Shein, is a juggernaut that has taken the industry by storm, where it has captured a 20% market share.[3] In 2024, it generated an estimated $38 billion in revenue.[4] That's a two-third increase on the $22.7 billion it made in 2022.[5] Customers love the brand's low prices and high-speed delivery, but critics deride the firm for promoting wasteful consumption as its customers snap up and quickly discard its cheap clothes.[6] Shein's shipping model is integral to its success, but it is also a big source of carbon emissions, which grew by 56% between 2021 to 2022, and by another 81% between 2022 and 2023, thus leading the company to officially become the biggest polluter in fast-fashion.[7] The company uses a direct-to-consumer model through air freight out of China, since discounted shipping rates and trade laws exempt packages with goods valued at less than $800 from tariffs if they are shipped directly to consumer homes.[8] This model saves Shein and its customers tons of cash.

Shein's business success leads to an inevitable conclusion: For Shein's shoppers, looking good at affordable prices and showcasing their hauls on TikTok is their primary goal. For them, and for Shein itself, sustainability seems to take a back seat.

To be fair, Shein has a few initiatives, like its Responsible Sourcing Program, that go beyond compliance, such as starting a platform to buy and sell used clothing. Still, most of the firm's actions are distinctively Operator. The company set up a "circularity" fund worth more than $200 million to inject cash into firms that are working on new sustainable fabrics, and these actions appear to be designed to placate regulators, sustainability advocates, and other stakeholders (e.g., government).[9]

OPERATORS RECAP

Operators make only marginal investments in sustainability beyond compliance. They do only what's necessary, which tends to be a narrow set of sustainability initiatives.

Goal and Role of Sustainability	Rationale
• Sustainability goal	Risk mitigation—They must pursue sustainability to stay in business—keep their "license to operate."
• Role of sustainability in customer value propositions	Marginal—They believe that most customers have no willingness to pay for sustainability—it is not an important differentiator.

Sustainability Strivers

Unlike Operators, Strivers specifically target the subset of customers who care about sustainability. But, for a variety of reasons, they're hesitant to shift their overall strategy and instead make tactical investments that supplement their existing strategy while also addressing market demand. Think of it like a person adding vitamins to her diet to fill in any gaps in her nutrition. Sustainability is like a multivitamin for Strivers, an add-on rather than a fundamental shift in diet.

Why this mindset?

Companies commonly choose a Striver approach if they believe that their core value proposition is already compelling and they don't want to compromise it—but they also see the opportunity in a sustainability augmentation. Imagine a company makes chocolate that is beloved by its customers for its taste and texture. If the firm is reluctant to modify its recipe or processes, it can do a few peripheral things that enhance sustainability while leaving the core product unchanged, such as switching to ethical sourcing, recyclable packaging, or green energy for manufacturing. These changes can attract more Green customers without affecting the core product or the loyalty of its existing customer base.

Strivers also use product extensions to add sustainability without changing the brand's core proposition. They may take this approach because they see the market as limited or uncertain and, as such, believe that extensions can stabilize or grow it.

Either way, we have seen many firms pursue these approaches. The grooming products giant Gillette, for example, introduced the "Planet KIND" brand line that includes razors packaged in 85% recycled paper with handles made from 60% recycled plastic.[10] These are much like Gillette's other razors, but with green elements swapped in or added on top. The brand has also partnered with Plastic Bank, a social fintech company dedicated to preventing plastic pollution of oceans. Gillette's promise to consumers is simple—"every Planet KIND product purchased will prevent 10 plastic bottles from entering the ocean."[11] Core customers can still get Gillette's standard razors, but Green customers who may have avoided the standard offering now have the option of an equivalent, and more sustainable, alternative.

Another reason companies choose the Striver route is because they see an inherent conflict between their current business model and a more sustainable approach. Examples include the soft drink industry, which relies heavily on sugar and plastics, or firms in the technology sector who depend on obsolescence of their products (we're thinking Apple here) and believe that making them more sustainable by extending their lifespans will cut into sales and profits. For Apple, augmenting the product with, say, recyclable materials or packaging can add marginal sustainability while leaving the core product, and its business model, intact.

Impact on customer value

It should be clear that while the Strivers' approach may enhance the firm's social profile and boost the reach of its offerings to some new customers, this creates only limited new customer value. After plotting the Strivers' approach on our investments vs. value chart (see figure 1-3), we end up with a scattershot of projects that shows random correlation between the degree of investment and the value created.

FIGURE 1-3

Striver mindset and customer value

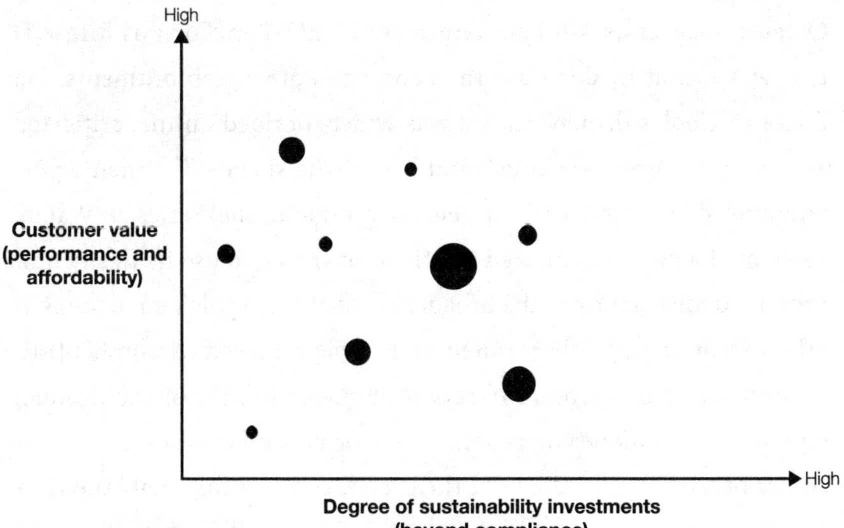

Note: Each black dot is a sustainability initiative (e.g., product R&D, process improvements, corporate social responsibility). More dots indicate more initiatives (or scope).

Let's return to Apple. With 2024 revenues of $391 billion and a net income of $94 billion, it remains one of the world's most valuable companies.[12] Yet despite its significant investments in sustainability, Apple remains a Striver.

The company has committed to becoming carbon neutral by 2030 and touts the fact that 22% of the materials used in products sold in 2023 were recycled or renewable.[13] But, given the seeming (some would say overt) planned obsolescence of its products, the company has struggled to make a convincing case about its commitment to sustainability. French regulators, for example, have accused Apple of intentionally making it hard for third parties to repair its products with generic parts.[14] And in-house repairs are costly—which could force consumers to upgrade rather than fix their devices.[15] One member of UK's parliament put it this way in 2020: "The charges proposed for repair by Apple in particular can be so expensive it is more economical to replace the item completely."[16]

Hoping to reclaim the narrative, Apple launched an ad featuring Octavia Spencer as Mother Nature (and CEO Tim Cook as himself) that was meant to showcase the company's green commitments. No doubt to Cook's dismay, the ad was widely derided online, criticized as "cringey," "greenwashing," and "all virtue signals."[17] When Apple announced its "first carbon-neutral product," the Series 9 Watch, some media outlets criticized the firm for trying to use its flashy new product to distract from the broader truth about Apple's environmental shortcomings.[18] Others noted that Apple achieved carbon neutrality only by using carbon offsets for about 20 to 25% of the product emissions.[19] Monique Goyens, the director-general of a European consumer organization, called out the brand, commenting that "the EU's recent decision to ban carbon neutral claims will rightly clear the market of such bogus messages, and Apple Watches should be no exception."[20]

STRIVERS RECAP

Strivers make more investments in sustainability than Operators—albeit mostly tactical investments that leave their overall strategy relatively unchanged. They launch many sustainability initiatives to raise their profile.

Goal and Role of Sustainability	Rationale
• Sustainability goal	Market opportunity and social capital—Participate and capitalize on an important trend opportunistically and build social capital by showcasing various initiatives
• Role of sustainability in customer value propositions	Peripheral value driver—It augments a value proposition and serves as a "minor" additional differentiator

Sustainability Enthusiasts

Ask anyone to name the greenest and most socially conscious brands they can think of and most will tick off a list of usual suspects—Ben & Jerry's, Seventh Generation, Tom's, Burt's Bees, Danone (prior to current CEO, Antoine de Saint-Affrique), Unilever under Paul Polman and Andy Jope, and their ilk. For brands and companies like these, strategy has a strong focus on sustainability. Sustainability drives corporate priorities, decision-making, culture, operations, marketing, R&D—essentially, every aspect of the firm. They genuinely make Right to Stay and Right to Win sustainability investments.

These are Enthusiast firms whose broad scope of initiatives and big investments in sustainability flow from the core belief that a singular focus on sustainability is not only the right thing to do, but will ultimately lead to superior firm performance—handsome revenues, profits, shareholder value, and market share. Enthusiasts aspire to become their industry's undisputed sustainability leaders and see this strategy as a differentiator and main source of competitive advantage. If you produce the most earth-friendly and socially sustainable soap, detergent, ice cream, or apparel, then the world, and investors, will beat a path to your door. As Unilever's Polman put it: "Shareholder value is the result, not the goal" of deep sustainability commitments.

Why this mindset?

Enthusiasts pursue their single-minded strategy for three broad reasons. The first is a sense of moral obligation to be part of the solution to the world's social and environmental problems, rather than an exploiter of global resources, as so many firms are. True Enthusiasts—from the CEO on down—reject shareholder capitalism, the notion that the primary social responsibility of a business is to maximize profits and shareholder return.

This doesn't mean that Enthusiasts are naive about business imperatives. They fully understand that an Enthusiast approach is only viable if the company is profitable. But, unlike their shareholder-capitalist competitors, they believe that the primary social responsibility of business is to generate social and environmental good. Do that and profits will follow.

This belief—and the second reason Enthusiasts pursue their strategy—derives from the conviction that there's a huge market opportunity in sustainable goods to be tapped. It's a bit of a "build it and they will come" mentality. In fact, as we've discussed, there *is* a significant segment of Green and a few Blue customers out there who will reliably reward firms for their environmental and social-equity efforts (we will return to this simple segmentation in the next chapter). It's consumers like these that keep the premium-priced sustainable stock at Whole Foods flowing. But the actual consumer demand for sustainable goods is certainly less robust than the evangelists believe it is. The say-do gap is widespread and persistent.

Finally, Enthusiast leaders believe a sustainability-first approach can be transformative for the firm itself, helping to build and sustain a culture that creates competitive advantage. In her influential book *Reimagining Capitalism in a World on Fire*, Harvard economist Rebecca Henderson argues that firms that put a sustainability purpose at their center have better alignment, trust, and motivation.[21] Alan Jope, Paul Polman's successor at Unilever, put 20,000 people through purpose training, believing that "companies with purpose last, brands with purpose grow, and people with purpose thrive."[22] According to Jope, firms that are sustainable improve employee engagement, retention, and productivity.

Certainly, on paper, the Enthusiast approach can look compelling. And indeed, there are a few examples of sustainable offerings that are highly profitable (think Patagonia) because they are mainly targeting niche customers. But in practice, our research finds that an uncritical embrace of Enthusiast strategy—where every product must have green credentials or a social purpose—can become a value-diluting managerial distraction. To be sure, brands must have a purpose—a reason to exist. This purpose does not always need to have social or green credentials, as Bernard Meunier advises.

Impact on customer value

As figure 1-4 shows, when we plot sustainability investments against customer value, we get another scattershot picture. So, yes, Enthusiasts can innovate sustainable offerings that create substantial new value for customers—those dots in the figure's upper right—things like convenience and lifestyle/image, both of which are offered by Chinese EV

FIGURE 1-4

Enthusiast mindset and customer value

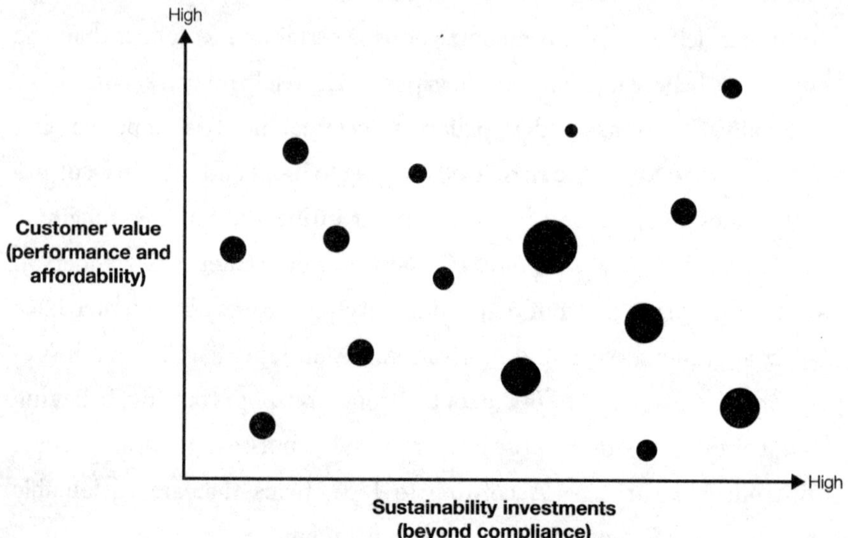

Note: Each black dot is a sustainability initiative (e.g., product R&D, process improvements, corporate social responsibility). The total number of dots is the scope of sustainability initiatives.

company Nio. But these successes come at the cost of a lot of wasted investment, those offerings on the lower right that sapped corporate resources and yet yielded little new value for customers.

Let's look at one of the less familiar Enthusiasts, the Waltham, Massachusetts-based consumer products company Preserve. Preserve is committed to changing "the way products are designed, made, used, reused, composted and recycled."[23] Few companies can match its sustainability credentials.

Founded by Eric Hudson in 1996, Preserve has one mission—to make products that are good for the planet and people. Hudson observed that more people were recycling in the United States, but few manufacturers were using these materials. He began with toothbrushes made from recycled plastics and expanded into razors, reusable containers, cutting boards, and compostable products such as plates and bowls. Preserve today proudly calls itself an "Environmentally focused lifestyle company" and sells recycled and plant-based products to its customers, who it calls "Preservers."[24] It's not a big company—revenue is estimated to be about $50 million annually—but it's as green as you can get. As with other Enthusiasts, sustainability comes first in everything the firm does.

Preserve wants to grow by going big on sustainability. "We never compromise on the ideology [of sustainability], but we may not go as far as we may like to," says Deanna Becker, Preserve's director of Stakeholder Operations. "We must balance our costs like anyone does. So, we may pick the next-best option, but we will always hold out our ideal choice as our guiding star."[25]

Driven by this mission, Preserve takes ambitious actions for a niche firm. It has recycled over 11 million tons of plastic waste to make its products.[26] It has a dedicated program for recycling ocean plastics called POPI (Preserve Ocean Plastics Initiatives). It donates 25% of revenue from POPI products to non-profits dedicated to cleaning oceans. It was among the first to become a certified B Corp organization in 2011—and sits in the top 5%–10% of certified B Corps for creating sustainability impact.[27]

But Preserve considers its own actions to be just the start. It wants to spread its enthusiasm to other firms. In 2023, Hudson articulated his vision for the industry. "We want other companies [including competitors] to be doing what Preserve does," he said. "We want other companies to be focused on reducing their footprint . . . so we help. . . . And generally, we think that a wider breadth of products that have these [sustainability] attributes is what consumers need, what Preservers need, [and] it's what the Earth needs."[28]

What Preserve is doing is, of course, great for the planet. But what value do they offer to their customers on top of "being green"? Does the compostable or reusable tableware work better? Do the knives provide superior cutting capabilities? Can we get them at a lower price? Their complete catalog fails to provide any of these answers.[29] It is quite clear that both performance and price are not evident reasons for buying Preserve products.

ENTHUSIASTS RECAP

Enthusiasts put sustainability at the center of their firm. They adopt an organization-wide approach to it. They invest heavily in sustainability—and try to have a big impact in multiple sustainability areas.

Goal and Role of Sustainability	Rationale
• Sustainability goal	Be the leader in sustainability. Use sustainability as the North Star and transform the firm.
• Role of sustainability in customer value propositions	Differentiate on sustainability. Build value propositions centered on sustainability in the belief that you can do well by doing good.

Sustainability Resonators

Last, we come to Resonators. These are the companies that ask, "How do we drive more customer value by being sustainable?" (see figure 1-5). These are firms like Schneider Electric, Siemens, Nespresso, John Deere, and Reckitt. You'll be hearing more about each of these and many others in the chapters to come.

The reverse is also true. Firms can choose to invest in initiatives that improve traditional benefits while also having a positive impact on sustainability. Sustainability is a driver of innovation and a catalyst for it.

Let's take a concrete example of a conventional sustainable product—an eco-friendly laundry detergent—and contrast it with a Resonator offering that delivers both enhanced performance *and* superior sustainability benefits.

Consider detergent manufacturers that take the conventional approach to sustainability. These companies will often start with a materiality

FIGURE 1–5

The Resonator mindset

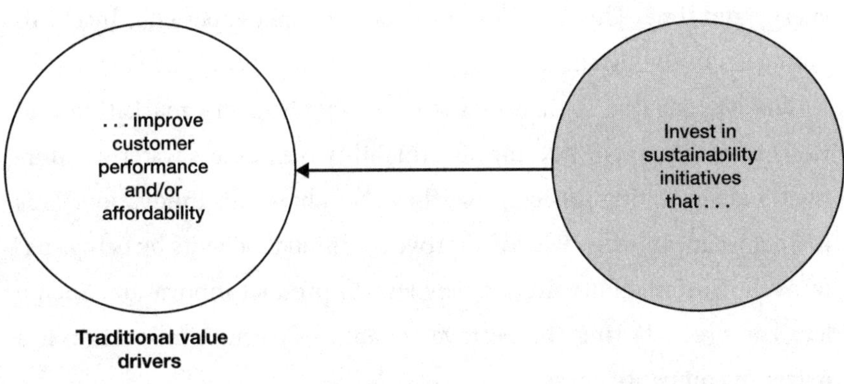

matrix to identify ESG issues that are important to the firm and its stakeholders, and then prioritize investments to address them. For laundry detergents, typical ESG concerns include the use of plastics in packaging, water use during manufacturing, energy use in the supply chain, labor practices of a supplier, and the presence of harsh chemicals in the detergent formula. Armed with these insights, detergent makers have developed new packaging that uses less plastic, developed formulas that require less water to make, switched to renewable energy sources in manufacturing, improved the vetting of suppliers' labor practices, and launched bio or plant-based products that reduce the use of problematic chemicals. A lot of their marketing messages highlight these elements of sustainability.

Let's now look at a Resonator's approach to the same problem. They will no doubt identify the above issues and act on some of them. But they also know that a customer's willingness to pay depends on delivering meaningful value as well. Ariel detergent creates new value by cleaning effectively even in cold water. This can reduce energy use during the wash cycle by 60%, thus reducing emissions and saving customers money. This sustainability innovation saves time and reduces energy use as well as wear and tear on the washing machine. Finish dishwashing detergent, with improved ingredients, is so effective that customers don't need to rinse dishes before they put them in the washer. This saves them, on average, 57 liters of water every dishwashing cycle, as well as energy and time. This also improves the customer experience by eliminating an annoying chore.

The bottom line is this: It was only when Finish's marketing and R&D team began considering sustainability (i.e., excess water use during the dishwashing process) that they thought of this innovation. This is what we mean when we say improve traditional benefits by being sustainable. Sustainability gives a new lens to product innovation. Such a lens can create lasting competitive advantages because innovation is a driver of competitiveness.

While saving customers' time and money are typical Resonator goals, Resonators think more broadly than that. In the coming chapters, we'll show the breadth of Resonators' sustainability-focused approach to innovation through a range of cases—how, for instance, Liechtenstein-based Hilti created a new business model that improves customer productivity; Nespresso supported farming practices in conflict-ridden regions that has enabled the launch of unique coffee selections; Schneider Electric improved customer efficiency through software and data solutions; Michelin introduced Product as a Service business models that enhance fleet fuel efficiency; and Revier Cattle rethought internal and supplier processes to improve the taste of beef.

Why this mindset?

While the Resonator path seems intuitive, it is hardly commonplace. Fewer than one in five firms innovates to improve sustainability.[30] All in all, just 10% of the companies we've studied qualify as Resonators.

In our research we've identified three key reasons companies pursue the Resonator path. First, they are genuinely innovation- and customer-centric to begin with, and as such, their approach to *sustainability* innovation is naturally customer-oriented. This is less obvious than it might sound; many firms are not particularly customer-focused in their innovation, seeking instead to address firm goals like "how do we become a digital leader" or "how do we seize more market share?"

Second, some companies find their way to the Resonator approach because it naturally aligns with their traditional value proposition. The German firm GEA, for example, makes manufacturing equipment for the food, beverage, and pharmaceutical sectors. The company became a market leader because its equipment is resource efficient. "We do not strive to improve efficiency and conserve resources just for the sake of it—rather, it is part of our corporate DNA," says Jurgen Mackel, a vice president. "We have always been working toward achieving the goals of better performance and more efficient machines," he notes. For customers, that means less machine wear and maintenance, as well as reduced energy and water consumption.[31]

And third, Resonators see sustainability innovation as a way to expand the scope of their products and services into new domains. As you've seen, sustainability opportunities often overlap with customer jobs-to-be-done. Farmers, for example, care about farm productivity more than equipment productivity. Understanding this, John Deere and Mahindra Group saw the clear links between farm productivity and more efficient use of resources by their equipment. Thus, they expanded into new domains: launching product/service offerings that reduced farmers' use of water, chemicals, and energy while increasing their productivity. Similarly, Schneider Electric, which we discuss below, saw a huge opportunity to think beyond simply selling energy-efficient equipment to thinking holistically about customers' energy management.

Impact on customer value

Earlier, we mentioned the breadth of Resonators' approach to sustainability-focused innovation—everything from product to process to

FIGURE 1-6

Resonator mindset and customer value

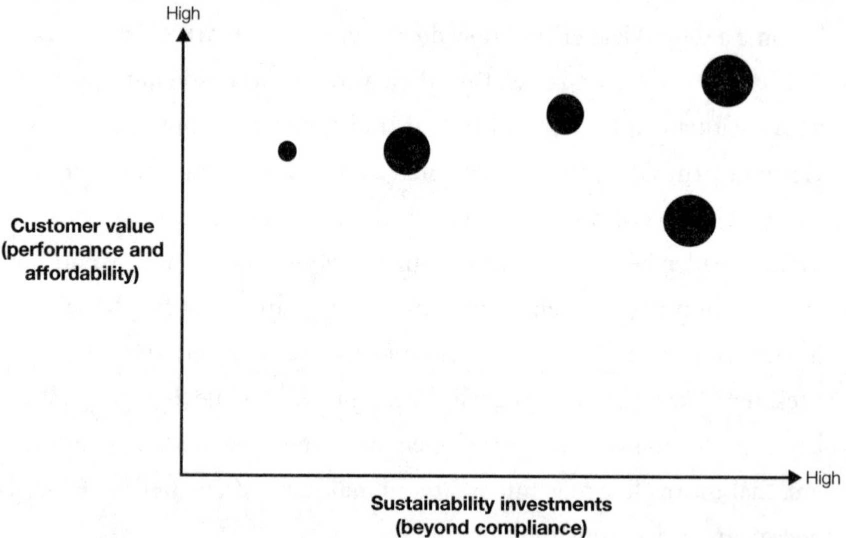

Note: Each black dot is a sustainability initiative (e.g., product R&D, process improvements, corporate social responsibility). More dots indicate more initiatives (or scope).

business model innovation. What these elements have in common is a commitment to customer value.

Figure 1-6 shows how this focus plays out. Resonators invest heavily in sustainability innovation, but always with the goal of value creation. The result is plotted above, showing that sustainability initiatives uniformly deliver improved performance, affordability, or both.

There may be some fortunate circumstances where the sustainability investment may not be large—those dots on the left—but still deliver high customer value.

Let's return now to the global energy-technology company Schneider Electric, a classic Resonator firm. In the early 2000s, Schneider recognized that reducing carbon emissions was becoming as important to companies as cutting costs. It saw an opportunity to provide a fundamentally new type of value to its B2B customers. Schneider shifted its focus from its traditional electricity-distribution offerings (such as relays and circuit breakers) to providing energy-efficiency services. Under the new model, customers needed only to purchase Schneider's integrated hardware and software solutions (such as smart thermostats that automatically lower the temperature when a building is unoccupied) to reap energy savings and emissions reductions. With this new strategy, Schneider's sales more than doubled over fifteen years and its stock price quadrupled.

Schneider's expansion into energy-management services continued in 2016 with the launch of EcoStruxure, an open digital platform that combines cloud-connected infrastructure, applications, analytics, and services.[32] The platform has helped the company further expand into energy consulting services, including real-time monitoring, decarbonizing, and complying with new energy regulations.[33] Through acquisitions of software capabilities (e.g., Aveva), venturing, incubation, and open innovation, Schneider Electric launched a suite of "Eco" services that provide dedicated expert and analytics support to help customer sites run more efficiently, including through the use of digital twin technology for infrastructure repair.

The company's focus on customer-value-creating innovation has fueled exceptional growth: In 2023, Schneider's revenue reached €35.9 billion with a net profit of €4 billion. Between March 2020 and August 2024, its stock price tripled. These gains come not only from shrewd business management, but also from disproportionate investments in innovation. Over the past decade, Schneider doubled its R&D budget. In 2023, the company increased R&D spending by 12.3% to over €1.2 billion per annum.[34] One result of these innovation investments has been a slew of sustainability awards (among them top ESG ratings from the Dow Jones Sustainability Index for thirteen consecutive years). But more to the point, from our perspective, is the direct impact these innovations have had on the company's performance: Schneider says the 74% of the company's revenues are deemed "impact revenues"—revenues it ties directly to solutions that accelerate "the energy transition and fighting the

RESONATORS RECAP

Resonators make deep investments in sustainability. They do fewer sustainability projects, with greater impact. They improve customer value by solving sustainability problems via different types of innovation.

Goal and Role of Sustainability	Rationale
• Sustainability goal	Create new customer value through sustainability innovation.
• Role of sustainability in customer value propositions	Sustainability is an enabler of differentiation on performance and affordability

climate crisis, while making a long-term positive impact on the planet and society."[35]

Clean Winners Build a Resonance Bridge

Operators, Strivers, and Enthusiasts represent very different sustainability strategies. However, as different as these strategies are, they focus on the same performance indicator—how much sustainability impact a firm can have through its sustainability investments. This can be expressed as the ratio of Sustainability Impact divided by Sustainability Investments (see left part of figure 1-7: "Societal value").

The goal of Operators is to minimize the sustainability investments in order to keep their license to operate. Thus, they tend to focus on the denominator—the resources invested into sustainability. Strivers want to "get the greatest bang for their buck," and they look at maximizing the return on their sustainability investments. Enthusiasts, by contrast,

FIGURE 1-7

The Resonance Bridge and ROSI

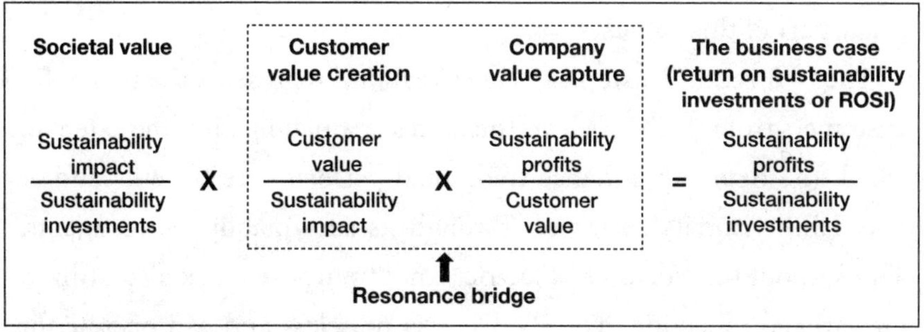

Note: ROSI: Return on sustainability investments.

focus on the numerator—this is because they want to be seen as leaders on sustainability.

Of course, Operators, Strivers, and Enthusiasts all make these investments because they *think* that they will pay off—*over time.* However, as we learned in the introduction to this book, this traditional approach to sustainability has a weak link to the business case. This link is weak because sustainability impact does not necessarily lead to a better market share or profit.

Clean Winners fixate on a different measure. Though the starting point is the same and the presumed end goal is the same—that is, market share or profits—their focus is on *customer value* that ultimately leads to market share and/or profits. Clean Winners are explicit in connecting the dots from their sustainability investments to business profits—we call this the Resonance Bridge (see figure 1-7).

Before going into the model's details, please compare the Resonance Bridge's tight logic with the model presented in the introduction (figure I-1) about "the business case of sustainability." We go from a loosely coupled, "box and arrow" model that "should" take place over time for "many different reasons" to the rigor of what is in a way a mathematical formula.

The Resonance Bridge is what Resonators obsess over. It consists of stubbornly asking two questions regarding sustainability investments: (1) How much value will they create for customers? (2) Can we appropriate part of this value?

The first ratio, "Customer Value Creation," represents the return for customers from the firm's investment in sustainability. It is the extent to which the firm can enhance traditional performance benefits and/or affordability for its customers through its sustainability investments. Think about the Volvo FM Electric, a multipurpose truck also utilized for garbage collection. The EV truck is noiseless and can operate for longer hours in Nordic cities that have restrictions on noise and carbon pollution.

Customer value creation is foundational for success, but it is also a means to an end. Firms need to be able to appropriate part of the value that they create for their customers. This is where the second ratio kicks in. "Company Value Capture" represents the incremental profits a firm obtains from creating the additional customer value.

This explicit connection makes it possible to compute a Return on Sustainability Investments (or ROSI), which is the ratio of a firm's sustainability profits from their sustainability investments (figure 1-7). Keep in mind that the sustainability profits are not the overall profits, but rather the incremental profits that come from a firm's sustainability investments.

What matters is understanding the extent to which customer value can be created through sustainability, and we will explore the three different ways this can happen. Before we do so, however, we must first do two things: question "common assumptions" about sustainability, and provide an overarching framework to guide the thinking. This is the object of the next chapter.

2

The Clean Winners Way

Resonance and Return on Investment

Brian was having a drink with his longtime friend Edward in their favorite café in Paris. "I am so happy with my new Mercedes," he said casually. "It's an electric car, and I bought it because I wanted to be sustainable."

You have probably heard similar sentences from friends, relatives, or colleagues. They seem innocuous, and if you were Edward, you would probably not challenge what Brian just said.

Read on. Now that we have introduced you to Resonance—the approach that tightly links sustainability and customer value, we explore in this chapter how firms use their Resonator mindset. This requires that we challenge five common beliefs and look at sustainability from a fresh perspective. As you will see, the first of these challenges directly addresses what Brian just said.

Clean Winners Confront Five Uncomfortable Truths

An explicit focus on value creation and value capture sets the right frame for scrutinizing the true role that sustainability plays in customer

TABLE 2-1

Conventional wisdom and uncomfortable truths

Common beliefs	Uncomfortable truths
1. Sustainability is a primary purchase driver	Sustainability *never* triggers purchases
2. Most customers care about sustainability and will prioritize it	Only one of three customer segments prioritizes sustainability; this is almost always the smallest segment
3. Sustainability features add value to customers	Sustainability features are perceived as a liability in some categories
4. Sustainability trade-offs are just like any other purchase trade-off	Sustainability trade-offs are unusual and difficult for customers to make
5. We can increase price by showing sustainability value to customers	The sustainability price premium is a myth; sustainability does not often directly result in higher prices

decision-making. In this chapter, we draw upon discussions and research with successful companies, as well as our own ideas, to draw the connection between sustainability and customer value creation. This research has enabled us to challenge five commonly accepted beliefs about sustainability (see table 2-1).

Let's examine each of these in turn.

Uncomfortable truth #1: Sustainability *never* triggers purchases

Think of buying as a two-stage process. In the first stage, a trigger causes customers to realize an unfulfilled need. This unfulfilled need—or in marketing parlance, the job-to-be-done (JTBD)—is the real reason for wanting a product or service. Functional or emotional benefits that fulfill this primary need are the "*Reasons to Buy*" (or RTBs).

For example, let's say a commuter finds public transportation too unreliable and cumbersome, which often makes her late for work (the trigger). She wants to show her boss that she is a diligent employee who takes her work seriously. She may conclude that she needs better and convenient transportation. She may consider purchasing an automobile because it provides reliable and on-demand transportation, thereby enabling her to be on time for work.

Take another example, that of chocolate bar maker Tony's Chocolonely. It has become a market leader in this category in the Netherlands. The company positions itself as a maker of "slave free" (meaning, no child labor) chocolate. But does a customer eat chocolate to save a child? No, the primary reason to buy has to do with pleasure. Notice that sustainability benefits play no role during the initial stage. The truth is that sustainability benefits *never* trigger a purchase because they do not fulfill primary needs.

The second stage involves a combination of discovery and evaluation. In this stage, sustainability benefits may become relevant for some consumers. We refer to these sustainability benefits as *Reasons to Care* (or RTCs).[1] Sustainability now becomes a self-imposed choice constraint for some customers. If the commuter cares deeply about the environment and she believes that EVs are better for it, then she will only consider all-electric vehicles.

The confusion about the real role of sustainability in decision-making arises because customers often express this two-stage decision process as a single-stage process, using statements such as "I chose an electric vehicle because I care about the planet," or "I buy fair trade chocolate because it has good labor practices." But, as we've learned, when a need is initially triggered, the customer's primary job is always satisfied by traditional benefits.[2]

Uncomfortable truth #2: Only one of three customer segments prioritizes sustainability; this is almost always the smallest segment

As every marketer knows, customers differ in their demographics, needs, sophistication, and, crucially, their values. This includes how they value sustainability. Green, Blue, and Gray customers differ according to their attitude toward a product's sustainability benefits in each product or service category.

- **Greens**—place a high value on sustainability in this product category, actively seek it in their purchasing, and may sacrifice performance or affordability for the sake of sustainability. They are willing to pay a higher price for it. Within the category of Greens, there are often Super-Green customers. These are devotees. They go the extra mile or are willing to make big sacrifices to be sustainable.
- **Blues**—place value on sustainability, but only under certain conditions. They prefer sustainable offerings over alternatives, provided they can make few or no sacrifices on affordability and performance. If they do need to make a sacrifice, they usually do so for an incentive—for example, a tax break—or, in the case of B2B suppliers, the ability to pass any extra costs to their customers. EV buyers in many countries have done so because of tax incentives. In Germany, for example, the moment the incentive was eliminated in 2025, EV sales plummeted by one-third from 19% of new cars purchased to 13%.[3]
- **Grays**—care little for sustainability. They don't consider it in their purchase decisions. There are also the Ultra-Grays within this category. These customers have a high dose of skepticism or even negativity toward sustainable offerings. They tend to avoid products with sustainable claims.

In the many sessions we have done with executives, including in Europe, we have asked the following question: "What is the highest portion of Green customers in the market for any of your product categories?" The highest numbers we heard were 10 to 15%. This cuts across both B2C and B2B firms and across many sectors. This percentage is a lot lower than we often see in surveys, which tend to measure intent, rather than actual behavior.

While customers may predominantly belong to one color, product-specific conditions may cause them to deviate from their general tendency. They may be a Green consumer in one product category (e.g., exclusively purchasing clean energy for their business), Blue in another category (e.g., preferring recycled packaging when it's convenient and if there is no cost penalty), and Gray in another (e.g., avoiding sustainable cleaning products or construction materials on the belief that their performance is not on par with conventional products).

A firm's first job is to assess the prominence of each group within their markets. This assessment must be ongoing because the proportion of Greens, Blues, and Grays may fluctuate, especially if incentives are introduced. There are several scales that firms can use to segment their customers according to their sustainability values.[4] Firms should select a scale that works for them, then stick with it so they can create consistent benchmarking over time.

Keep in mind that a customer's color in each category is likely the product of prolonged maturation, and therefore resistant to short-term change. Firms should be wary of trying to alter customers' beliefs about sustainability. If they feel they *must* try, they should accept that they can probably provoke only marginal changes, at most convincing a few fringe Grays to become Blues and a handful of outlying Blues to become Greens.

Uncomfortable truth #3: Sustainability features are perceived as a liability in some categories

Can you think of instances where the mere signal of sustainability may prove to be a burden? There are many, and this phenomenon is called "sustainability liability."[5]

As we have seen in chapter 1, sustainability liability occurs when claims over sustainability reduce customers' perceived value. This arises when customers believe that sustainable products have inherently lower performance. This perception is widespread in categories where "strength" is a valuable attribute. For example, customers might assume that a bio detergent is less strong at removing stains. This is because environmentally friendly products are associated with gentleness—which implies they might struggle to tackle tough stains.

When researchers labelled soap dispensers in one airport lavatory as organic, they found that visitors consistently used more of it per handwashing than identical—but unlabeled—soap in another lavatory in the same airport.[6] The conclusion was that customers *assumed* organic soap to be weaker or, perhaps, gentler. Consciously or subconsciously, consumers assume certain sustainable products perform less than their non-sustainable counterparts.

As another example, consider plant-based meats versus natural meat. The tagline for Beyond Steak—a vegan alternative to beef—is "Now steak tacos are good for you." The messaging focuses on the (claimed) health benefits of the product. But consumers might assume a sustainability liability and wonder if Beyond Steak is hiding something—that it tastes inferior to real steak. Or they could be skeptical of the claim because plant-based meats contain artificial ingredients.

Sustainability liability manifests differently across demographics and social strata. Research shows that males are less likely to be Greens or receptive to sustainability messaging because they often associate sustainability with femininity.[7] Indeed, claims of sustainability cause some men psychological discomfort. Furthermore, sustainable lifestyles are often linked—consciously or subconsciously—with nonconventional lifestyles. Bud Light learned this lesson the hard way, when it faced a massive backlash and lost its market-leading position when it created an ad campaign with transgender spokesperson Dylan Mulvaney.

The reverse of sustainability liability is true as well. In gentler categories (such as body lotions, or taste), consumers tend to think naturalness (i.e., no chemicals) enhances the product quality. Natural body lotions are gentler on the skin. Organic meat is tastier. In these categories, sustainability is an asset.

Our advice to firms is simple. Don't assume that adding sustainability is a positive. You must understand your customers deeply, especially those that are Gray. If a firm is not careful, its sustainability efforts can come to naught because it may be perceived as a liability.

Uncomfortable truth #4: Sustainability trade-offs are unusual and difficult for customers to make

Buyers are used to making trade-offs when they purchase products. They'll pay a higher price to get higher quality, for example, or they'll accept the risk of having to return clothes that don't fit in exchange for the convenience of buying them on the internet. These are conventional trade-offs (i.e., "I give this up and I will get this"). The "I" here can refer to an individual, a company, or easily identified beneficiaries, such as friends, relatives, or coworkers.

Unlike the subset of products that are both more affordable and perform better—a group we discuss in detail further on—many sustainable products require trade-offs, such as a price premium for organic ingredients. While this might seem like a conventional trade-off, it is not. Many sustainability trade-offs are atypical (i.e., "I give this up for someone unknown or for society at large"). For instance, when customers are asked to pay higher prices for fair-trade goods, they are being asked to make a general contribution for the welfare of society—for example, for the equitable treatment of workers in Bangladesh. These workers are "distant beneficiaries" because buyers rarely see or meet them. Similarly, when buyers are asked to reduce meat consumption to cut emissions, they are asked to make a sacrifice today so future generations can experience the payoff down the road.

Complicating customers' cost-benefit analysis, the true benefits of a product's sustainability can be difficult for customers to authenticate, such as whether a chocolate really is "100% slave-free."[8] Or if an "eco-conscious tube" is actually better for the environment.[9] Many customers rightfully question sustainability benefits because of exaggeration and rampant greenwashing. A 2022 article in *Harvard Business Review* suggests that greenwashing is at an "industrial scale."[10] This article found that 42% of green claims in Europe are false, deceptive, or exaggerated. We will talk further in chapter 7 about greenwashing and communication strategies.

Uncomfortable truth #5: The sustainability price premium is a myth; sustainability does not often directly result in higher prices

Let's see what firms routinely do in practice. While estimates vary, a New York University report on US consumer-packaged goods shows that sustainability-marketed products typically command a 28% price premium.[11] This is already a steep price increase. A report by the consulting firm AT Kearney—across different product categories, including fashion, beauty, and healthcare—shows that sustainable product prices are often 75% to 85% higher than those of conventional products.[12] Are these premiums justified? Will most customers accept them?

Firms that charge a price premium for their sustainable products provide three justifications for higher prices. The first is that sustainable offerings cost more to provide. Farmers who grow organic crops often have a lower yield, a higher cost, or both, and will thus need to be compensated accordingly. The second is a lack of economies of scale in the production and delivery processes. And the third is that the firm is bringing additional value by bringing additional sustainability benefits.

But who determines a product or service's value? Simply put, it's the customers—and only them. Value equals the net benefits that customers perceive. Firms can offer additional benefits, but if customers don't see their worth, they won't pay for them, and the cost is wasted. Companies may find this frustrating after investing in new features to stand out from competitors and might suspect customers of bluffing for discounts. However, generally, firms shouldn't resent customers for their perceptions.

Viewed from this lens, only Greens and some Blues will value sustainability benefits and may pay more. Grays and most Blues won't value them and will only notice the higher price, making the sustainable product less attractive to them. This often means price premiums will be rejected by most customers.

We are not saying here that sustainability offerings that charge a premium cannot succeed; many can when they demonstrate value. We discuss this at length in the next chapter.

The uncomfortable truths suggest the need for a new approach to sustainability

If there is an underlying theme to the uncomfortable truths, it is that sustainability matters *selectively*—that is, not all customers care about it, it is not a purchase trigger, nor is it a satisfier of primary needs, it is a liability in some product categories, and customers must often make difficult, uncomfortable trade-offs for it. The uncomfortable truths lower the role and true potential of sustainability.

The implication of this selective appeal is that firms should cast aside the notion that a firm should optimize on sustainability—it is not, and should never be, the end goal. They should ignore the advice from the numerous books or articles that advocate putting sustainability at the center of their business. If you put sustainability at the center of your business, the danger is that your focus will be on sustainability and not necessarily on customers. This is a trap!

If putting sustainability at the center is not a great idea, then what is? Based on our research and consulting with many Clean Winners, we have developed a framework that captures the essence of this more selective, customer-centric approach to sustainability. Our framework "repowers" sustainability by putting customer-back innovation at the center of sustainability efforts. We will share our framework with an example.

The Framework

We will use the example of East-West Seed (EWS) to illustrate our framework. EWS, with revenues of approximately $250 million in 2024, was founded by Dutch entrepreneur, Simon Groot in 1982. Groot's family had been in the seed business for over 200 years in the Netherlands. During his travels to Asia, Groot saw that smallholder farmers in tropical regions were in a vicious cycle of poverty and malnutrition.

Groot set up EWS's headquarters in Thailand with the mission "to provide innovative seeds and services that help improve the livelihood of tropical vegetable farmers and promote sustainable farming and business practices."[13] The company first introduced a hybrid variety of bitter gourd (bitter melon) and soon followed with crops like pumpkin, cucumber, and other Asian gourds. These, along with corn, onion, tomato, papaya, and hot pepper, are now among its popular products with small holder farmers.

Let's look at the role EWS and other parties play in creating customer value. EWS represents the Firm in figure 2-1. Its own activities and collaboration with suppliers and partners (e.g., dealers) enable it to provide farmers with seeds and support services. Other firms (figure 2-1) often

FIGURE 2-1

Role of various players in the value chain in customer value creation

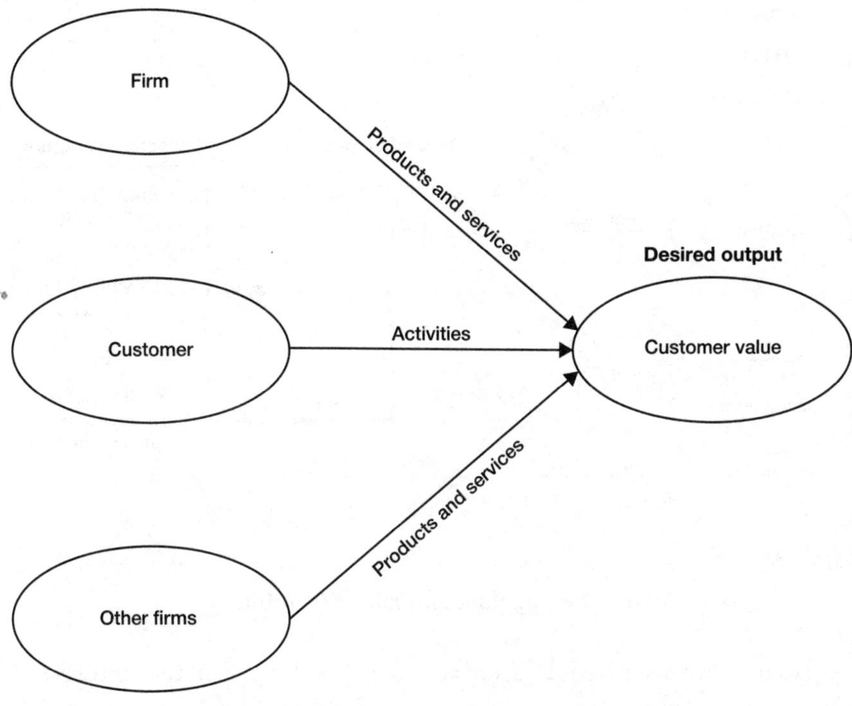

play a role in helping customers as well. Applying these roles to the example of farmers, these other firms provide products and services that complement those of the Firm (EWS), such as watering equipment, fertilizers and pesticides, planting and harvesting equipment, and consulting advice to farmers.

Farmers (i.e., the Customer in figure 2-1) play a crucial role in the entire process. Their own activities and practices have a major impact on "customer value," which for a farmer is typically yield (in other words, productivity). The higher the yield, the greater the income for a farmer. And of course, there is the environment in which a customer operates. Farming is the world's largest outdoor factory. Weather can be a boon to, or play havoc on, a farm's yield.

FIGURE 2-2

Sustainability innovation and customer value

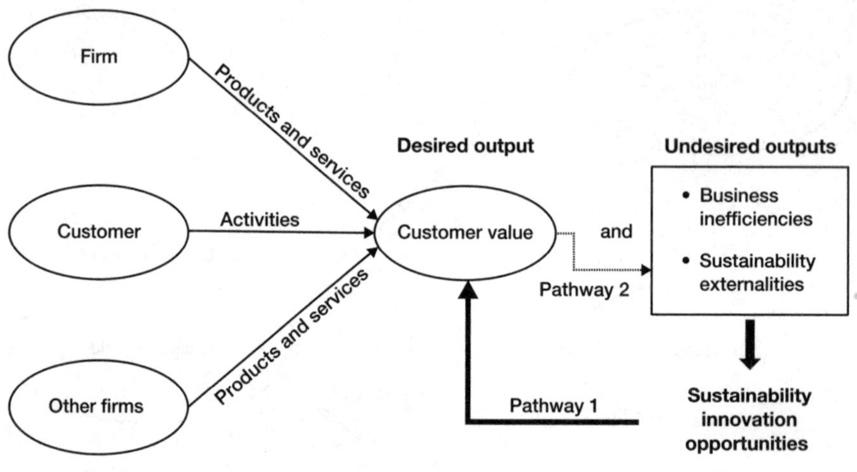

Leveraging sustainability innovation

Up to now, we discussed the set of actors that participate in the entire ecosystem as producers of a desired output—customer value. Think of this desired output as an essential "muscle" of the body. For a farmer, this would be yield.

As good as the intentions of all parties involved in the value creation process may be, there are often unproductive practices that result in undesired outputs (see figure 2-2). Most firms did not pay much attention to them in the past. Think of these unwanted outputs as "fat." It is waste. It is a harmful side effect that was produced either intentionally or unintentionally.

There are two types of undesired output—business inefficiencies (waste) and sustainability externalities (harmful side effects).

Business inefficiencies by the actors involved in the entire ecosystem contribute to waste in the value creation process. A firm that is bureaucratic, underutilizes its employees, or has poor quality inspection processes creates waste and additional costs to the system. Similarly, a business that uses untrained labor will have unproductive waste or suboptimal results.

Sustainability externalities, both environmental and societal, are the second type of undesired outputs. EWS, for instance, will have Scope 1, 2, and 3 greenhouse gas emissions from its operations and logistics. These have harmful side effects. The sustainability externalities can arise directly while creating customer value, or indirectly from a firm's business inefficiencies. For example, a farmer's neglect of soil or excess use of fertilizers are inefficient practices that have harmful effects on the environment.

Resonator firms are particularly good at putting a spotlight on these business inefficiencies and sustainability externalities. These undesired outputs provide a lens for creating *new* customer value. Resonators use innovation to find solutions to reduce these undesired outputs (see Pathway 1 in figure 2-2). But they do this innovation with intent. They explore two fundamental questions: "How can the firm leverage sustainability to increase value for customers?" and "How can the firm leverage sustainability to decrease business inefficiencies?" Sustainability is a catalyst of innovation. By decreasing inefficiencies—that is, getting costs out of the system—they have the option of making their products more affordable to customers.

In the long run, because innovation that leads to higher customer value is a source of competitive advantage, Resonators strengthen their innovation edge and competitive advantage over other firms.

You will notice in figure 2-2 that there is a second pathway. Pathway 2 goes from customer value to sustainability externalities. This is a fortuitous path. Even if a firm is not thinking of sustainability, it nevertheless reduces externalities simply by improving customer value. For example, a company may improve its packaging to keep its products fresh. This simple act reduces spoilage, which has negative sustainability externalities.

EWS's founder and current leaders, CEO JC Filippi and COO Dilip Rajan, recognized these inefficiencies and externalities across the value chain. The firm has invested heavily on "sustainability innovation opportunities" to design new products and services. By taking a sustainability lens to improve customer value (yield and income), they have rolled out a massive knowledge transfer effort to improve farmer practices. Of EWS's 2,800 employees, 7% are involved in knowledge transfer to help farmers with better crop planning, pest/disease management, post-harvest support, climate-smart techniques such as crop rotation, reduced chemical usage, and cover cropping. In 2023, EWS directly improved the practices of over 167,000 farmers.

Addressing known inefficiencies through sustainability innovation is vital, but can a firm innovate beyond these known inefficiencies? Absolutely. Think of these as "unrecognized opportunities." These may be problems that a customer does not recognize or cannot articulate. For example, what if a farmer is not using the best available seed, fertilizer, or pesticide?

This is another area in which EWS made significant strides. The company has twenty-two R&D centers in nine countries, with a main goal of using a sustainability lens to improve farmer productivity and yield. It's R&D division realized a long time ago that many tropical areas were suffering from water shortages or poor soil conditions. Using natural grafting processes, EWS's teams have developed seed varieties that use less water with no compromise in yield. It has seed varieties that are pest resistant, but blossom better than regular varieties. Such innovations have a major impact on a farmer's input costs and yield. These activities make EWS a Resonator.

Steepening the Innovation Trajectory

Recall chapter 1, where we argued that most firms are Operators. This reality was quantified by IBM. Its study of 5,000 global executives showed that bosses' spending on sustainability *reporting* exceeded spending on sustainability *innovation* by 43%.[14] This shows the scale of the leadership challenge. Clean Winners lead their firms away from mere sustainability compliance—and toward sustainability innovation. They get a sustainability innovation lift.

Why is this shift important? Because companies often fall into the trap of complacency. GEA, a German firm that makes equipment for the food and dairy industry, has always focused on energy efficiency. Its implication was that it could continue to improve energy efficiency and thus claim sustainability. But doing so would simply be business as usual. Its innovation trajectory would be unchanged (see figure 2-3).

Yet two of GEA's leaders were unsatisfied with more of the same. CEO Stefan Klebert and CSO Dr. Nadine Sterley challenged the organization to find new ways to foster a step change in energy efficiency and reduce other undesired outputs. They put GEA on an accelerated innovation path (figure 2-3). We call this the sustainability innovation lift. This innovation acceleration would not occur but for GEA's leaders recognizing that sustainability can be a catalyst for innovation.

FIGURE 2-3

Illustrative sustainability innovation lift

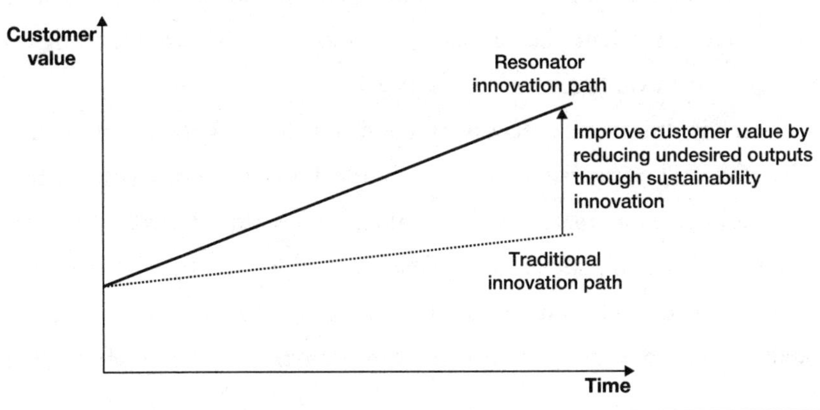

As an example, GEA's innovation acceleration led it to introduce the "Add Better" label on new products that are *significantly* more resource-efficient than their predecessors.[15] Its marine separator, for example, uses up to 9% less energy, while a water saving unit reduces the cooling water consumption for separators by 100%.[16] The company now has more than thirty products carrying the Add Better label.

The Real Implication of Innovation Acceleration

We are often asked if a firm is better off being an Operator and doing the minimum on sustainability, or better off becoming a Resonator. After all, an Operator could invest its money and resources elsewhere and getter a better return.

This seems like a legitimate argument, but we believe it is flawed. Why?

Our argument is simple. An Operator firm would likely continue its normal trajectory of innovation (see figure 2-3). This is expected because in most firms, radical innovation occurs occasionally. Most of the time, a firm is engaged in incremental innovation.

On the other hand, a Resonator firm changes the trajectory of innovation by paying attention to sustainability—that is, being more mindful of undesired outputs. Since innovation is a source of competitive advantage, any firm that accelerates innovation is strengthening its competitive advantages.

There is, however, a necessary condition for a firm to obtain this advantage. The undesired outputs should be large enough that when reduced, they can create customer value. This is almost always the case. There is plenty of waste around. We are surrounded by inefficiencies. Indeed, when Eccles and Serafeim analyzed the business practices of 3,000 firms, they discovered something remarkable. They found that firms that *steepened the trajectory* of their innovation improved both their commercial *and* sustainability returns.[17]

Let's take two simple examples.

Consider online retail in the United States. Ecommerce returns in the country contribute significantly to material waste and reduce retailer profits. Some 17% of online purchases were returned in 2023—$743 billion worth of returns.[18]

Horizon Pulp & Paper is a market leader in sack kraft paper, a durable paper type used widely in packaging. The firm exports its product to more than seventy countries.[19] Its direct customers are "converters"—firms who fashion the paper into packaging. The converters sell the packages to ecommerce firms, who use them to ship products to consumers. These paper packages often get damaged during the shipping process—and cannot be reused. Because of this, the ecommerce company must send (or include) a *second* package so consumers can return unwanted purchases. This increases the cost to the Ecommerce firm and creates unnecessary material waste.

Horizon has no contact with consumers. Yet despite this, its marketing department demonstrated great leadership. Its marketers researched the consumer need and uncovered the need for a durable, multi-use pack. Horizon found a way to reformulate the pulp in the paper to make the package more durable. The material costs of the package remained the same for the company. Yet the improved durability allowed a package to be used multiple times. This allowed Horizon to maintain profitability and price while significantly reducing waste. Its enhanced offering was more attractive to ecommerce businesses that got the dual benefit of reduced costs and favorable environmental impact.

OCP Group, the fertilizer company with over $11 billion in annual revenue, took a slightly different path to Horizon. OCP performed an analysis of the negative externalities stemming from fertilizer. Its examination revealed that 54% of nitrogen in fertilizers escapes into the atmosphere, leading to waste, extra costs for farmers, and environmental harm.

Rather than treating this as an unavoidable inefficiency, OCP redesigned its product strategy by developing customized fertilizers tailored to specific soil conditions. This customization meant that the right fertilizer would be used at the right rate, at the right time, and in the right place—the so-called 4Rs of nutrient stewardship.[20] The shift improved maize yield in Ethiopia by 37% while reducing price and improving soil health and the environment.[21] By prompting the firm to innovate on sustainability, OCP's leaders have transformed it into a Resonator in this product category.

What's Coming Next?

Our book examines how firms can use a sustainability lens to accelerate their innovation that creates customer value. It flips the traditional question of "how can we be more sustainable?" to "how can we leverage sustainability to create customer value?"

In the next part of the book, we introduce three ways in which Resonators leverage sustainability (see figure 2-2). We refer to them as "Resonance Pathways." Each pathway focuses on one player in the value chain—the left part of figure 2-2.

Chapter 3 examines how a firm can use sustainability innovation on its own products and services to create greater product value. We refer to this pathway as *Product Resonance.* Chapter 4 focuses on the firm's customers, and more specifically, on how they use its products and services. Identifying usage inefficiencies is an important pathway to create both customer value and reduce the customer sustainability impact. We refer to this pathway as *Usage Resonance.*

Product and Usage Resonance offer innovative approaches to integrating sustainability into a firm's existing product markets, thus addressing the "how to win" strategy. Chapter 5 examines the "where to play" strategy, encouraging firms to explore new growth opportunities by analyzing how other firms serve their customers. This approach identifies inefficiencies and externalities that enhance customer value. We refer to this pathway as *Strategic Resonance*.

PART TWO

THE PATHWAYS

3

Product Resonance

Taking a Hard Look at New Offerings

As Louis looked at the new outside door that her neighbor Grace had bought for her flat, he noticed the little sustainability logo on the top. Curious, he remarked, "I see you bought a door with great thermal insulation. That's a great choice for the planet. Congratulations for becoming more sustainable." Grace responded, "What do you mean, Louis? I didn't notice the logo; I simply bought the door because it is going to save me money, nothing more."

In the previous chapter—through our discussion of uncomfortable truth #2, "The Buying Blueprint"—we shared that a product's sustainability benefits (Reasons to Care, or RTCs) have unique characteristics that differentiate them from traditional benefits (Reasons to Buy, or RTBs). Unlike RTBs, RTCs never trigger a purchase on their own and they often require non-conventional trade-offs. This means that RTCs should be considered a distinct category of benefits—a breed of their own.[1]

Yet beneath this distinction lies a critical point: It's easy to assume that RTCs are always an add-on benefit—an additional way of increasing value beyond an offering's traditional benefits. This is a dangerous assumption, and we have seen many firms make it.

The right way to think about RTBs and RTCs in the value equation is to examine the interaction between them. As we'll see, this has important implications for firms pursuing Resonance strategies.

The Three Pathways

Sustainability benefits can interact with products' traditional benefits—the attributes that attract consumers in the first place—in three distinct ways:

- **Independence**—traditional benefits are *unaffected* by sustainability benefits
- **Dissonance**—traditional benefits are *diminished* by sustainability benefits
- **Resonance**—traditional benefits are *enhanced* by sustainability benefits

These models can apply to any type of B2B or B2C product or service with sustainability benefits.

Understanding a sustainability offering's perceived Independence, Dissonance, or Resonance is critical for value creation. Firms that fail to understand these three relationships may pursue a marketing strategy that's poorly aligned with their offering's interaction type, thus sabotaging it in the marketplace. Conversely, if they correctly understand the situation, firms can develop a winning playbook for each interaction. However, this does not mean that the three playbooks have the same potential. As we will see, Resonance offers the best opportunity to leverage sustainability. This is the pathway on which Clean Winners rely—Product Resonance.

We acknowledge that firms may follow different trajectories in their longer-term sustainable product strategies. They may well start with Independence and Dissonance and only get to Resonance after a few new product iterations. As an example, we will discuss the iconic case of the Toyota Prius in this chapter.

To illustrate the three interaction types, let's start with a baseline example: a classic detergent lacking sustainability benefits. We call this "Regular" detergent.

In our example, consumers regard this Regular detergent as a middle-of-the-pack product. It does a good enough job of cleaning clothes and removing stains. It is moderately gentle on fabrics, but this attribute plays a minimal role in customer perceptions. The detergent gains an average score on its traditional benefits; a zero score on its sustainability benefits; and, as it is priced in the low to midrange, a high score on affordability (see figure 3-1).

FIGURE 3-1

Regular detergent with no sustainability benefits

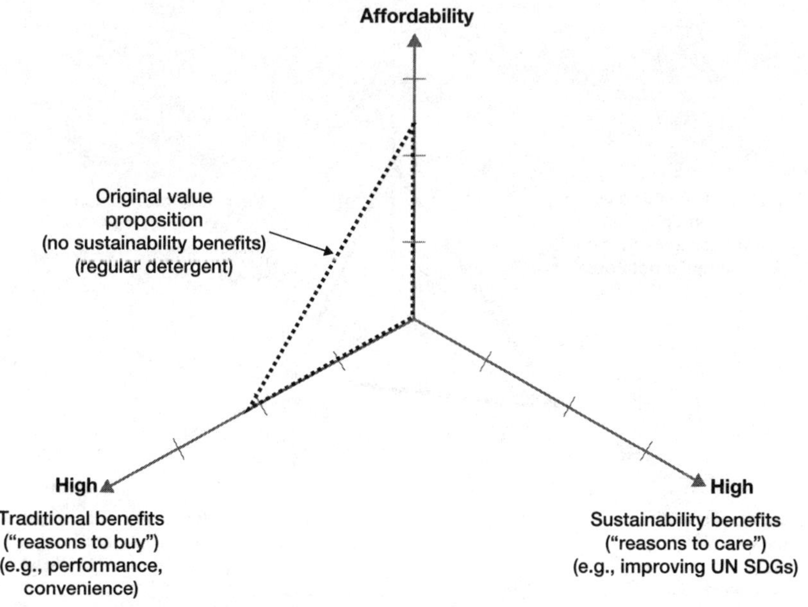

Note: UN SDGs: United Nations Sustainable Development Goals.

Adding sustainability benefits to this product leads us down three different pathways, which we'll explore in turn.

The Independence pathway

The first alternative is a detergent with packaging made of a new material that can be either composted or recycled. We call this product GreenPack detergent. GreenPack is priced slightly higher than the Regular detergent because its sustainable packaging is more expensive to manufacture. This eco-friendly packaging does *not* affect the detergent's traditional benefits—its cleaning ability, stain-removing power, and gentleness. There is no change to the traditional benefits or RTBs. This is a case of *Independence*. The customer gets the *same* performance of the traditional

FIGURE 3-2

Independence case: GreenPack detergent vs. regular detergent

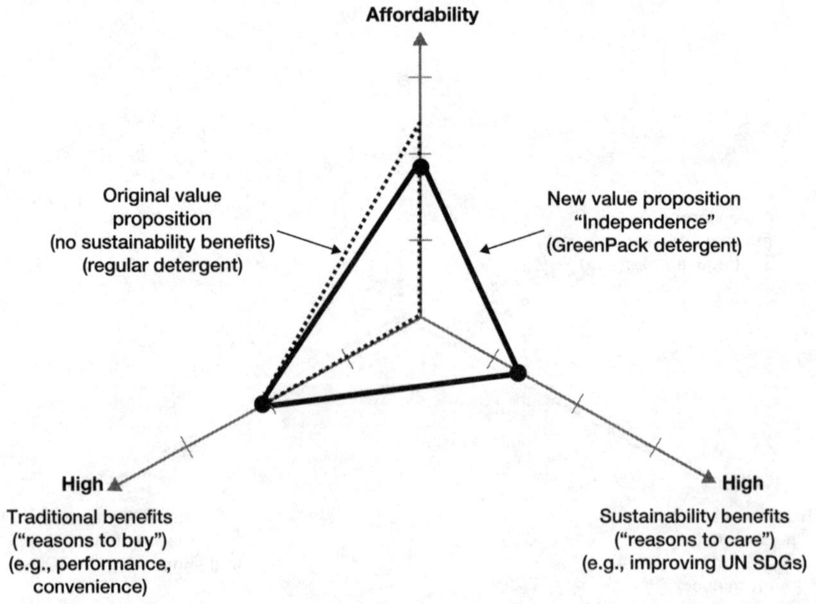

Note: UN SDGs: United Nations Sustainable Development Goals.

detergent with an added environmental benefit that has no impact on performance—but at a slightly higher price. Although in this example we show a price increase, this decision is entirely in the firm's hands.

The graphic compares GreenPack's benefits (solid black lines) with the Regular detergent (dotted lines) (see figure 3-2).

If we look at the size of the two triangles representing the value propositions of the detergents, it is easy to believe that the GreenPack detergent has a superior value proposition. However, ask yourself this question: Would a Gray customer care about the sustainability benefit? The answer would be no. In reality, once we eliminate the sustainability benefit, we quickly realize that for Blue and Gray customers, the Independence Pathway presents customers with a sustainability/price trade-off: "We can help you meet your sustainability goals, but it may cost you more." This becomes a problem from an adoption perspective.

Let's illustrate this with some real-world examples.

As part of its overall sustainability strategy, Unilever has long championed the fight against food waste. Through a variety of partnerships and educational programs, the company has leveraged its popular Hellmann's mayonnaise brand, using an Independence strategy that generates sustainability benefits that are unrelated to its primary benefit—its taste.

Hellmann's changed its packaging to become more sustainable and made a commitment to reducing food waste. These initiatives have no impact on the core offering—the quality, versatility, and flavor that make it a popular mayonnaise. But the brand's fight against food waste gives a subset of consumers a reason to care, which is an add-on sustainability benefit unrelated to the brand's core benefits.

On the B2B side, consider Solvay, which manufactures chemicals using green energy. That should have no impact on the performance of the chemicals. Similarly, Maersk, the Danish shipping and logistics giant, is the first large shipper to deploy methanol-fueled vessels.[2] This is certainly a welcome move for Maersk customers, as it enables them to decarbonize their supply chain, thus reducing their Scope 3 greenhouse gas emissions. The performance of Maersk ships is unaffected by the change of fuel. The methanol-enabled seacraft are as fast as the equivalent conventionally fueled vessels.[3]

Let's now turn to a more detailed look at how an Independence strategy affects pricing. While independent offerings may generally cost somewhat more than their traditional counterparts, they are unlikely to justify a fat price premium. That's because in addition to the classical competition among firms who get the same customer "job" done, Independence players now face a new type of competitor on the sustainability side. They are now competing with *all firms* who can help the customer become more sustainable—irrespective of the primary job the customer bought the product to do. Let's return to Maersk, which traditionally competes in the shipping industry (with the likes of CMA CGM and Hapag-Lloyd) to win, say, Volkswagen's business. Now, firms like Michelin, Bosch, or CATL become Maersk's competitors too—because just as Maersk helps VW reduce emissions in its supply chain, any one of these firms can also help Volkswagen accomplish the same goal.

Volkswagen can compute the cost of a kilo of CO_2 emission reduction across *all* its suppliers.[4] It can then decide how to allocate its sustainability dollars in the most efficient manner. Who knows? Maybe buying low rolling resistance tires from Michelin will deliver VW the greatest bang for its buck—for now. If that's the case, the fact that Maersk's shipping is methanol-fueled no longer confers an advantage—and therefore pricing leverage—in its competition for VW's business.

A similar thing happens in the B2C sector. This is because consumers often have limited "sustainability" budgets. Thus, organic beef competes for the consumers' sustainability dollars with a diverse basket of goods—such as ethical chocolate, natural laundry detergent, and organic linen. Consumers will generally be unwilling to pay a sustainability premium for every product they purchase. Their calculus might run like this: "Since I already helped the planet by paying extra for organic beef and milk, I don't need—or cannot afford—to buy expensive natural laundry detergent too."

Market research demonstrates that Greens and some Blues are genuinely interested in sustainable offers. However, when they are confronted with the offer—and its price—they often realize that they could make better use of their sustainability budget. Firms with Independence should consider their pricing strategy carefully, mindful that even a small premium may push even committed customers away.

In turn, this reveals that firms pursuing Independence strategies would be foolish to anticipate large price premiums. If they want to serve the mass market, they will probably only be able to command a modest premium. This does not mean that the Independence playbook cannot be successful. It can be a gainful enterprise—provided firms are realistic about the size of the market (some of the Blues and all the Grays will be uninterested) and, most importantly, about the premium the market will bear. In general, Independence offerings asking for a hefty premium is a surefire path to reduced sales volumes.

The Dissonance pathway

To explore the second pathway, let us return to detergent as an example. Now imagine that, in a second alternative formulation, the product only uses natural, plant-based ingredients. This shift somewhat diminishes the detergent's stain removal performance versus traditional chemical ingredients.[5] This new formulation—which we call Bio detergent—suffers from *Dissonance.* Consumers understand that the detergent is eco-friendly, but also suspect that it may underperform and realize that it costs more than the Regular detergent. Thus, reasons to care increase, but reasons to buy decrease (see figure 3-3). This creates a difficult

FIGURE 3-3

Dissonance case: Bio detergent vs. regular detergent

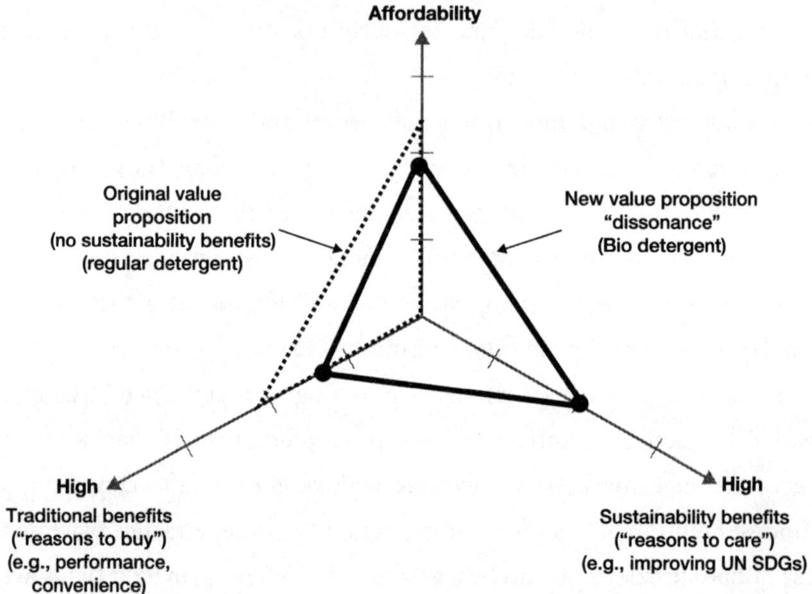

Note: UN SDGs: United Nations Sustainable Development Goals.

trade-off. In exchange for sustainability benefits, customers must sacrifice some degree of both performance and affordability. Only Greens would seriously consider accepting this offer.

Figure 3-3 compares Bio detergent's benefits (solid black lines) with the Regular detergent (dotted lines). The traditional benefits (RTBs) are diminished when sustainability benefits (RTCs) are introduced. Because there is a negative relationship between sustainability and traditional benefits, we call it Dissonance.

Bear in mind that product performance is often measured across several dimensions, as different customers seek different benefits. When buying shoes, for example, some customers might prioritize style and aesthetics, others support and comfort, still others durability, grip, and aeration. In B2B manufacturing markets, the same principle applies.

Consider the market for compressors. Some customers seek maximum power, while others prize energy efficiency. Still others might focus on durability or compactness. As a result, a product may be dissonant for one customer, but not for another.

In evaluating a product's Dissonance, it can be useful to divide it into three subgroups: full, mixed, and perceived. Understanding the distinction between these will be important to companies in determining whether a dissonant offering can (and should) be shifted toward Resonance.

Full Dissonance occurs when performance along one or more traditional value dimensions diminishes without any increases on other value dimensions. To return to the footwear example, someone might buy a pair of shoes primarily because the brand has a reputation for durability and, secondarily, because that model uses sustainable materials. Unfortunately, the alternative materials make the shoes slippery on wet surfaces without enhancing any other traditional benefit—comfort, breathability, and so on. Such a situation is a case of Full Dissonance.

By contrast, *Mixed Dissonance* occurs when there is an increase in performance on at least one value dimension, despite a decrease in performance elsewhere.

In the motorcycle market, for example, Harley Davidson's electric Livewire motorcycle faced Mixed Dissonance. The firm's initial ambition was to sell 100,000 bikes per year by 2026.[6] However, it only sold 687 LiveWires in 2022, and 305 in 2023.[7] The decrease only continued, with just 99 sold in Quarter 3, 2024.[8] Electric motors can offer faster acceleration and torque than their conventionally fueled predecessors. Yet, for many Harley diehards, the bike's green attributes may detract from key reasons to buy—the traditional bikes' macho reputation and unmistakable roar. What's more, concern about the bikes' range and the limited availability of recharging spots compromises the sense of unfettered freedom Harley owners' prize. Here, the advantages conferred by electrification are outweighed by the losses perceived by Harley's traditionalist customer base, leading to Mixed Dissonance.[9]

There are situations where merely signaling that a product is eco-friendly can generate negative impressions among customers; this is where we can have instances of *Perceived Dissonance.* For example, environmentally friendly drain openers may be perceived by consumers as less effective, even if that's not really the case.

Dissonance of any type might seem like something firms want to avoid. Yet it does not necessarily mean these offerings will struggle in the marketplace or fail entirely. Indeed, in terms of pricing, it can offer some good news. Remember that Green customers are highly committed to sustainability and are often willing to pay a premium for sustainable offers. Thus, if the firm is realistic about true market size and if the sustainable offering is economical to produce in the small volumes the market will bear, the Dissonance pathway can be successful.

With the right strategy, firms can profitably sell dissonant products to Greens. And while expanding beyond the niche market of dedicated Green consumers is challenging, it is possible.

One strategy to broaden the customer base for a dissonant offering is to attract a subset of Blue customers—those who care somewhat about sustainable aspects of offerings—who can be convinced to accept a performance sacrifice because they stand to gain personally from new benefits that are tied to a firm's sustainability actions.

Oatly, a Swedish firm which makes milk from oats, has grown beyond a niche market by rethinking consumer needs and cleverly repositioning around them. The firm was founded in 1994 as a plant-based alternative for consumers who were lactose intolerant. In the early years, its sales were languishing. But, in 2012, Toni Petersson, the new chief executive, and John Schoolcraft, creative director, repositioned Oatly as a lifestyle brand for the "post milk generation"—"It's like milk, but made for humans."[10] This repositioning was crucial because most consumers consider plant-based milk alternatives as having a different—often inferior—taste and nutrition profile to milk.[11] Oatly touted its sustainability credentials, but its main message to consumers focused on how

Oatly should be part of their trendy lifestyle.[12] This made any compromise on taste or nutrition—be it real or perceived—palatable to a broader audience in Europe. Oatly entered the US market in 2016 and the company is now valued at nearly $850 million, with 2024 revenues of $820 million.[13]

Companies with non-sustainable offerings can create dissonant sustainable-product extensions or sub-brands to expand their reach with Greens. Toyota's hybrid Prius, launched in 1997, is an iconic example.[14] However, the Prius was expensive and some considered it underpowered compared to mainstream rivals.[15] Yet the greenest buyers were willing to make those trade-offs for the environmental benefits it promised.

Toyota smartly used non-market strategies to broaden the Prius's appeal in California.[16] It lobbied the state legislature to allow the Prius in high-occupancy vehicle lanes even with a lone occupant. Buoyed by environmental groups and the state legislature, Prius owners were allowed to park for free at public meters in Los Angeles and other Californian cities. These types of non-market strategies pulled in Blue customers. Over time, Toyota improved the Prius to narrow the trade-offs on traditional benefits. In 2024, Toyota sold 4.14 million hybrid vehicles globally across its brands.[17] To put this number in perspective, Ford sold 2.03 million vehicles of *all types* in the United States that year.[18]

Provided a firm is realistic about the segments and market size for its dissonant offering, and about its customers' willingness to accept sustainability trade-offs, it can effectively deploy its marketing resources. This should include ongoing scans for potential converts—identifying customers who previously resisted a dissonant offering, but are now willing to accept some sacrifice to achieve their sustainability goals.

The Resonance pathway

To explore the third pathway—Resonance—let's return to the detergent example. This final formulation, PowerWash, uses a natural ingredient

FIGURE 3-4

Resonance case: PowerWash detergent vs. regular detergent

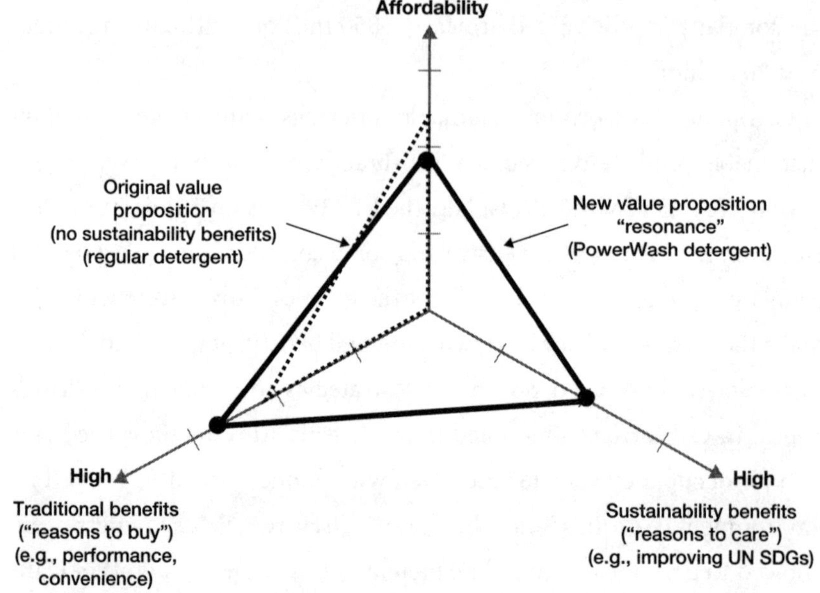

Note: UN SDGs: United Nations Sustainable Development Goals.

that improves stain-removing properties and gives the product a unique odor-fighting power. While its ingredients may make it more expensive than its non-sustainable competitors, it works better than them. This is a case of *Resonance,* in which sustainable features enhance a product's performance. Resonance purposefully leverages sustainability to increase customer value.

The graphic in figure 3-4 compares PowerWash's benefits (in solid lines) with the regular detergent (in dotted lines).

Resonance clearly creates a compelling competitive model by bringing both volume potential and opportunity for price premiumization to firms. Resonant products can target the broadest customer base. A price premium is possible because Resonance offers address a customer's job-to-be-done (JTBD) better than competing products. Because of this, the brand message can be made compelling to all segments. *The real power of Resonance products is that they make sustainability optional—the firm can choose to talk about sustainability or not at all to make a sale.* This is the reason for the broad appeal across Green, Blue, and Gray customers.

There are four types of Resonance: Classic, Accrued, Partial, and Economic. These are determined by the price paid by the customer.

Products with *Classic Resonance* offer sustainability benefits and better performance than competitors, but at the same price as the non-resonant alternatives.

You'll recall the case of Finish dishwashing detergent from the introduction, a perfect example of Classic Resonance. Dishwashing, even with a dishwasher, used to be a chore. Before the dishes could be stacked into the machine, they had to be rinsed. Dishwashers and detergents often weren't up to the task of cleaning them otherwise. But pre-rinsing is wasteful, using up to seventy-five liters of water per wash, compared to just ten liters used during the machine cycle itself.

Many firms communicate on the efficiency of their dishwashing detergent without pre-rinsing. However, Finish's technicians designed a dishwasher tablet so effective that they claim it uniquely removed the need for pre-rinsing. Whether Finish customers care about sustainability is largely irrelevant: The detergent saves them time and reduces their water bills. And Finish was able to increase its sales volume by 11% and regain market share.

Accrued Resonance occurs when some dimensions of performance increase and the purchase price rises, but the latter is compensated by the fact that the total cost of ownership falls. In this scenario, wise firms will pitch the sustainable alternative as an investment. The success of an Accrued Resonance offer depends on two key factors: the length of the payback period and its perceived uncertainty. Sometimes, the savings are linked with the price of the inputs, such as energy, raw materials, or water.

Consider Electrolux. It is a leading manufacturer of washers that harnesses a Resonance effect in its product strategy. The company has developed a "cushion-like" care drum that is gentler on garments and significantly reduces their wear and tear.[19] The ability to wear clothes longer appeals to all customers—irrespective of their sustainability beliefs—for both emotional and functional reasons. These are clothes that people like wearing—they want to maintain their initial look and feel. Furthermore, prolonging the life of their clothes helps consumers save money. The traditional benefits are clear.

Yet the Electrolux care drum also delivers sustainability benefits to Greens and Blues. The company calculates that if the lifespan of clothing could be extended by nine months, it would reduce carbon, waste, and water footprints by 20 to 30%. This is particularly relevant given the rise of fast-fashion clothing, which quickly wears out and is often discarded after a few wears. Buying an Electrolux care drum is one way to fight the $100 billion fast-fashion industry. It might cost more than an ordinary alternative, but the benefits—both traditional and sustainable—accrue over time, eclipsing the initial extra outlay.

Curries, part of Swedish Group Assa Abloy, provides a B2B example of Accrued Resonance. Curries is a US manufacturer of steel door and frame openings. Its QMax door core is an alternative to the traditional polyisocyanurate and polyurethane materials.[20] QMax is more expensive than its conventional competitors—but it offers increased thermal insulation, which provides over 20% energy savings, a traditional benefit wanted by all customers. In addition, QMax is 100% recyclable. It also offers a 22.7% carbon footprint reduction. These are sustainability benefits that Greens—and some Blues—will relish.

Partial Resonance occurs when some dimensions of performance increase and the price paid by the customer rises, but the latter is not offset by reduced cost of ownership. Despite a higher price, these offerings still provide great benefits to customers under the right circumstances. These are classic differentiated offers: They deliver better performance in exchange for a higher price.

Take, for example, the Revier Cattle Company. This is a fifth-generation family farm in Minnesota. It has a simple message: "If you like our taste today, you will like it tomorrow." Its beef is consistently tender and flavorful, and it's priced accordingly. In 210 blind tastings with chefs, restauranteurs, and butchers, the company's products were preferred to similarly graded beef on 209 occasions. How does Revier do it? The consistent, superior taste would not have happened without the farm's sustainable practices.

Tom Revier, the company's chief executive, created a program called Total Livestock Care. The program focuses on excellent feed (all natural and with no preservatives, hormones, or additives) and excellent facilities (to reduce stress on cattle). These practices have improved the taste—a key reason to buy. They also enable the company to achieve an enviable sustainability scorecard compared with the industry average: 73% lower greenhouse gas emissions; a 12% reduction in fuel use; a 40% reduction in groundwater usage; and a 32% healthier cattle herd.

But Revier does not have to sell these additional sustainability benefits to customers. The superior taste of the product does that itself. Rather, the sustainability benefits are a bonus for those who desire them—customers for whom "all natural" is compelling. Revier might cost more than standard beef, but it performs better—both in terms of traditional benefits (taste) and sustainability.

Economic Resonance is the last type of Resonance, where added sustainability benefits contribute to a decrease in purchase price while leaving traditional performance constant—or in some cases, they increase it. Holcim's Durabric is a block used for construction in Africa that is made of local earth, sand, cement, and water. Unlike traditional clay bricks, it does not need firing. These blocks have more compressive strengths than bricks (traditional benefits). They also reduce the CO_2 emissions by a factor of 10 and reduce the cost of wall construction by 20%.[21]

Achieving Product Resonance

Achieving Product Resonance is hard—there is no magic wand to make it happen. Recall figure 2-2 in the previous chapter, which suggests that there are two methods to achieve Product Resonance. It does matter which method a firm uses, and ideally it uses both. The first method begins with a focus on customer value *improvement*. This is about taking significant strides in helping customers with the JTBD. But the company does not look at value creation in isolation; they look at any unintended negative sustainability externalities as well. These externalities can come from both the firm and customers.

Let's take the example of an automobile insurance firm. If we're honest, the customer JTBD is to "never use the insurance product." Customers would love a product that prevents accidents, so they never have to go through the emotional trauma of life disruption and the inconvenience of making a claim.

An automobile insurance firm that excels at "accident prevention" would engage in actions such as improving driving behavior or providing incentives to purchase cars with more advanced safety warnings. Such actions would have a direct and enormous impact on reducing the negative sustainability externalities of both the firm and the customer. To put the impact in perspective, in 2023, there were nearly 41,000 deaths from automobile accidents in the United States.[22] Also, the cost to insurance firms in 2019 was $340 billion.[23] Imagine the benefits to customer physical and mental health, as well as the environmental savings to society from reduced waste!

The second method focuses on reducing unwanted outputs. A firm can reduce business inefficiencies that have negative sustainability externalities, or it can directly focus on reducing negative sustainability externalities. The key is not to blindly reduce these unwanted outputs, but to select those that will have an impact on customer value, which is depicted by the Pathway 2 arrow in figure 2-2. In the automobile insur-

FIGURE 3-5

Types of innovation projects

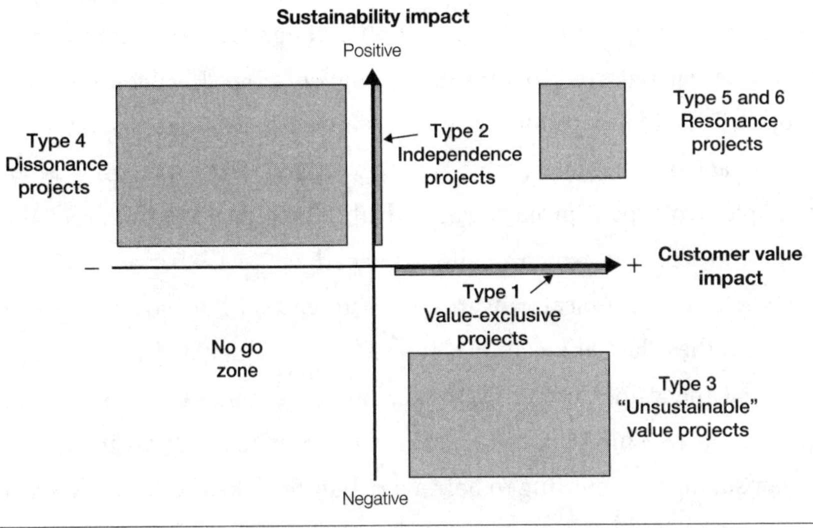

ance example, mitigating business inefficiencies by eliminating paper in the recruiting and claims process alleviates negative environmental effects while also reducing costs. Or, recognizing that after an accident, the environmental footprint and repair costs are unnecessarily high because too many body shops are taking the easy way out by simply replacing parts that can be repaired or refurbished. Reducing these costs can add value to customers by providing better pricing, and it can also benefit society.

A simple way to bring these two pathways together is to develop a simple map with two dimensions—Customer Value Impact and Sustainability Impact (see figure 3-5). A company can assess the impact of its various projects on these two dimensions. A shampoo manufacturer, for example, could undertake certain R&D projects, such as making lighter bottles, using recycled PET, developing a smaller lid, substituting plastic with carton-based packaging, developing refill solutions, creating a new bottle design, and developing a smart dispenser.

A company doing this mapping will soon realize there are six types of projects as shown in figure 3-5. Single-dimension projects are those that have an impact on either customer value or sustainability, but not both. Developing a more attractive bottle design with the same weight and same materials could be a possible example of a Type 1 "value-exclusive" project. Type 2 "independence" projects increase sustainability, but have no impact on customer value. Using recycled PET packaging is an example. Do type 2 projects ring a bell? These projects represent the Independence case, which we discussed earlier.

Type 3 and 4 projects advance one dimension, but have a negative effect on the other. For example, Type 3 "'unsustainable' value" projects increase the value to the customer, but have a negative impact on sustainability. Think about a "smart" dispenser that adjusts the quantity of shampoo according to hair mass, but the dispenser is made from plastics and uses disposable sensors. Type 4 "dissonance" projects create just that for its customers. Carton-based packaging, instead of plastic, creates Dissonance if it progressively deteriorates in the shower, even before the shampoo is fully consumed.

Type 5 and 6 "product resonance" projects, in both cases, are a win-win situation as they increase both customer value and sustainability. Examples would be a smaller, elegant lid, which makes the packaging more attractive while reducing plastics usage, or shampoo refills, which can be purchased either for sustainability or for customer value reasons. The distinction between the two types of projects is the causal mechanism: What was the initial project trigger (or intent)? Type 5 projects start with customer value—make the bottle more elegant by developing a smaller lid, which in turn reduces plastic usage. Type 6 projects start with sustainability—develop a more circular model, which in turn will bring more value to the consumer as the price will be lower.

While our project examples above are internal R&D projects, the same framework can be used for acquisitions. Alltech—which is in the animal nutrition business and has a commitment to "Working Together for a Planet of Plenty"—understood this.[24] Its acquisition of Agolin was a deliberate attempt to acquire a product with Resonance. Alltech's essential oil blend Agolin-Ruminant helps dairy farmers achieve better performance while improving sustainability gains. An objective study showed that when Agolin was used for over four weeks, it increased milk yield (+3.6%) and feed efficiency (+4.4%), and it decreased methane production from cows by about 8.8%.

A portfolio approach to achieve product resonance

Some firms have used a systematic approach to deliberately move toward Product Resonance. Sika, which makes bonding, sealing, and coating chemicals for construction and automotive industries, has made much headway toward Product Resonance over the past few years. With net sales of CHF 11 billion in 2023, Sika sells products that enhance the durability of building structures and make automobiles lighter and more efficient.[25]

Sika uses a standardized approach called "Sustainability Portfolio Management" to assess its entire product portfolio for sustainability and performance.[26] The framework ranks Sika's products on six performance-benefit criteria (cost, durability, aesthetics, technical performance, additional features, and application performance) and twelve sustainability-benefit criteria (e.g., air quality, chemical hazards, packaging, and climate). Using both assessments in combination, Sika places its products into six product classifications:

- Barriers (very low sustainable products, regardless of performance)
- Concerns (low sustainable products, regardless of performance)
- Neutral (neutral sustainability, regardless of performance)
- Low Performance, More Sustainable (i.e., Dissonance)

- Same Performance, More Sustainable (i.e., Independence)
- More Performance, More Sustainable (i.e., Resonance)[27]

The beauty of this categorization is that it quickly provides guidance for action. For products in the first three clusters, Sika must decide whether to improve them—or stop making them. We have already provided advice in this chapter on dealing with the Dissonance and Independence cases. The highest-ranked classification, "More Performance, More Sustainable," consists of Resonance products.[28] These products leverage sustainability to deliver better performance benefits. Through such a robust assessment system, Sika can prioritize products and innovation projects as well.

Through this classification, Sika found that some of its products had a large sustainability footprint relative to industry averages. They realized that a portion of them were overengineered. Such products had a negative sustainability impact because of the use of excess chemicals, while also unnecessarily increasing the costs for Sika and the final price for customers. The innovation team didn't just reduce materials, but made them better as well. This made the products more competitive with better functionality for the JTBD, and they were thus moved into the "More Performance, More Sustainable" category.

Don't ignore customer participation in achieving resonance

Many firms focus on delivering sustainability impacts by improving the environmental and social performance of their products, operations, and supply chain. A product made using clean manufacturing processes from sustainably sourced components delivers its benefits at purchase, as do fair-trade certified goods. While firms may invest a lot of resources in creating a clean supply chain, it is nevertheless passive from the standpoint of customers, because the sustainability benefits require nothing beyond the initial purchase decision.

But for many products, the real sustainability gains come after purchase and depend on customers' adoption of key usage behaviors—for example, running a dishwasher on the eco-cycle rather than the regular cycle, or recycling aluminum coffee capsules. In both cases, the firm must convince customers to change their post-purchase behaviors to generate the benefit—this can be seen as sustainability via customer participation.

This strategy asks customers to pitch in to support a sustainability initiative. The message to customers: "We're in this together and we need your help to deliver meaningful gains." The firm's role is to put a spotlight on a sustainability issue and make it easy for customers to change their behaviors in ways that help address it.

Consider Reckitt's Harpic, a leading toilet cleaner brand. In a world where one in three people have limited access to toilets, Harpic's purpose is "to provide safe, hygienically clean toilets for everyone, everywhere." The government of India spent over $30 billion to construct 100 million toilets.[29] But a majority became unusable because of poor maintenance and because many users preferred to defecate in the open. To address this challenge, Harpic targeted the "toilet deserters" with a media campaign based on social embarrassment. One message read: "The government spent 13,500 Rupees on a toilet you are not using." They used India's largest religious event, local events, Bollywood, and a door-to-door awareness campaign to obtain pledges on upkeep and sanitation. The program has reached more than 90 million people, improving both hygiene and brand sales. Today, one in three homes in India use Harpic.

Nike has had a long-standing support of women and girls in sports. Among its many programs are ones that target young girls, because by the age of fourteen, girls drop out of playing sports at twice the rate boys do. The company's Made to Play initiative works with community partners to increase girls' access to sporting opportunities, and the firm has invested in recruiting and training female coaches.[30] But as one Forbes contributor observed, "Empowering women athletes takes more than just inspired marketing. . . . It takes merchandise."[31] Nike has invested heavily in developing innovative sports gear for girls and women, and this has become an important revenue stream, growing from less than 10% of revenues in the 1990s to about 25% of its revenues today.[32]

One More Degree of Freedom

Let' s be clear. We make it sound like Product Resonance was easy, but of course it is not. Innovation and new product development are areas where companies fail—most of the time.

Simply put, firms need to fire on all cylinders to harness innovation, and we believe that sustainability could give them extra power on their path to maximize value for customers. The path we describe here, Product Resonance, is an additional degree of freedom. We have seen many firms who have discovered this path on their own, and we hope that this chapter is useful to our readers.

As discussed in chapter 2, Clean Winners can maximize customer value by looking beyond their products and services. The path we describe next, Usage Resonance, broadens this view to consider the way customers use these offerings.

4

Usage Resonance

Rethinking Customer Use

Isabelle parked the coupe outside her local café. Once inside, she buys a coffee and fires up an app. Scrolling down, she spots a silver convertible. "That will be perfect for the drive to the Cote D'Azur this weekend," she thinks. She clicks "deliver" and picks up today's newspaper from the rack at the side of the café. Thirty minutes later, a smartly dressed man arrives. "Ms. Morio?" he says. Isabelle raises her arm: "Hello!"

The man walks to her table and hands her some car keys. She exchanges them for the set in her handbag. "Thanks," she says. "Thanks," says the man, who then leaves. Isabelle finishes the article she was reading then walks outside. The coupe is gone. She presses the key fob and opens the door of a gleaming silver convertible.

Do consumers value products themselves or the services those products provide? What is more valuable, owning a nice car, or driving a different car depending on the conditions? Does anyone aspire to own a dishwasher or washing machine, or do they simply desire clean dishes and clothes? Wouldn't firms be better off simply buying compressed air instead of owning and operating their own compressors? So, rather than continuing to purchase products, shouldn't we all switch to buying their usage as services? This chapter focuses on Usage Resonance; it explores how current customers' usage patterns could be a formidable reservoir to reduce both business efficiencies and sustainability externalities.

Traditional business models—which rely on selling tangible products—typically rely on three assumptions. They assume that:

- The customer must own the product to have the right to use it.
- The customer-owner is responsible for the end of life of the product.
- The price a customer pays is independent of the realized performance of the product.

You might think about this and conclude that it is a rotten bargain. In return for buying the product, the customer—not the seller—assumes the greater risk. She must hope that she will use it sufficiently to justify the price paid. She is likely unable to alter the price if the product performs less well than she expected. It is her duty to safely dispose of the product when it expires.

Given the drawbacks to customers, one might wonder why traditional—product-based—models have persisted for so long. The answer comes from the realities of trade. The product-based model was ubiquitous, so customers had little choice but to accept the trade if they wanted to access the benefits of the product. From a firm's point of view, the traditional business model existed for good reasons. Companies were unable to ascertain how buyers used the product. This information asymmetry meant it was unrealistic to hold vendors responsible for the product's performance and return. As one Renault CMO said to one of us: "We cannot put a Renault guy in all of our Renaults." Hence, the legal principle dating back to the Roman Empire: "Caveat emptor" (let the buyer beware). Customers need to exert due diligence when they purchase goods; sellers have comparatively limited obligations.

Yet the world is changing. Rapidly. Digital technology—particularly the internet of things (IoT)—is transforming the seller-customer compact apace. You now have a Renault guy in every Renault because cars are connected—they talk to their manufacturers in real time. This is true of myriad appliances—from automobiles to elevators to thermostats.

In the IoT age, firms can access massive amounts of process and impact data. IoT provides evidence-based diagnostics data at low cost (and zero marginal cost). This has spawned *Anything as a Service* (XaaS) business models:

- The customer "simply" uses the product (as a service).
- The firm owns, operates, and maintains the product—and is responsible for its disposal at the end of its life.
- The price the customer pays may depend on the product's actual performance.

We are of course not the first ones to talk about XaaS business models. As we will see, these business models offer a trifecta of increased customer value, reduced inefficiencies, and improved sustainability performance. Potentially, customers win, firms win, and the planet wins. These business models represent a second path to Resonance that we call Usage Resonance.

The customer wins, as shown in our vignette at the start of this chapter. Isabelle can use different cars depending on her needs. Risks shift to the car manufacturer. She does not have to worry about the maintenance, insurance, and the resell of the cars she is using. In addition, if the contract entails a performance agreement (say, about the availability of car models), the price could be lowered—the car manufacturer has a vested incentive in making sure that it delivers on its promises.

Firms and sustainability win, if the preexisting "customer-owning" model was inefficient—which is very often the case. Consider two examples.

First, the automotive sector. How efficient is the traditional ownership model? Surprisingly, just 1%. Why? On average, a car is used one hour per day, about 4% of the time.[1] And during that hour, a vehicle designed for five often carries only 1.5 people, a quarter of its capacity.[2] A quarter of 4% equals 1%. This simple math underpins many businesses: taxis, rental cars, car-sharing platforms, ride-hailing services . . .

In fashion, the story is similar. Imagine you are buying a dress for a wedding. How many times do you wear that dress in the company of your friends? Once? Perhaps twice? By the third time, you worry that people might notice you wearing the same dress, and thus you become unwilling to do so. Soon enough, the garment goes out of vogue, and is relegated to the back of your wardrobe, perhaps never to be worn again.

Lemons can provide us with a good example of what happens in many industries. What do customers do when they want lemon juice? They run to the local grocery store, buy the available lemons, cut the lemons in half, squeeze the lemons with their hands to get juice, and throw away the two halves. How efficient is the whole process? To answer this question, let's compare this to what a firm would do. They would carefully select lemons and use machines to extract significantly more juice. They would also find markets for pulp and skin, as these ingredients could be used in cosmetics and detergents. And they could also use seeds to grow more and even juicier lemons.

It all sounds wonderful. So alluring is the idea that journalists and consultants tout such models as being the future of business. Yet the reality is that in many cases, Usage Resonance is in its infancy. The reality may be less appealing than the utopian headlines. There is persistent showcasing of the same small set of firms. The reality is that many firms struggle—and several have failed.

In this chapter, our job will be to segue from dream to reality: It is not so much the "whether," but rather the "when" and the "how" that we need to address.

The Usage Resonance Model

Shifting from "buying" products to "using" services is a simple but profound shift. Once one realizes just how inefficient current usage patterns currently are, the potential upside becomes clear. By changing their model, firms can make profound efficiency gains. And these gains are the best way to find sustainability gains—thus fostering Usage Resonance.

The existing types of misuse noted earlier give rise to three types of gain: misuse/overuse, underuse, and linear-only abuse. Each type of failure is an opportunity for future success.

Three categories of gain

MISUSE AND OVERUSE. Customers are rarely expert in the products they buy. Generally, manufacturers are more knowledgeable about their products than the people to whom they sell. The "Renault guy" likely knows how to drive and maintain the Renault better than the guy who owns it.

The lack of customer expertise has consequences. It leads to misuse—which leads to and includes overuse. When customers are responsible for a product they buy, they often use it suboptimally. They frequently maintain it poorly. This is not a criticism: It is simply the consequence of selling products to people who lack specialized skills, assets, or capabilities.

The home cook is unlikely to own an industrial juicing machine; he thus wastes much of the lemons he purchases. Few customers are expert in thermodynamics, so a good deal of the energy they buy to heat and light their homes and offices is squandered, because the buildings are inefficient, as are the practices of the people who use them.

In the B2B space, many machines require specialist skills to use them: Consider the operation of complex Valmet paper-pulp mills or BOBST labelling machines. Those who use them must be trained to do so. Similarly, buyers of complex machinery such as aircraft engines are challenged to maintain them.

Yet, when *manufacturer* expertise is introduced, great gains can be made. Rolls Royce provides Engines as a Service (EaaS) to the aviation industry. When academic researchers compared the performance of engines under an EaaS model to a traditional model, the results were astounding. Product reliability was 25–40% higher under the service model.[3]

In a similar vein, French motoring giant Michelin offers Tires as a Service (TaaS) to the haulage industry on a pay-per-kilometer model. Michelin handles tire maintenance, including "time-sensitive" operations such as tire permutation, regrooving, and retreading. Perform these operations too early and you forgo mileage and fuel savings—but doing so too late would also jeopardize hundreds of thousands of kilometers of use. By taking charge, overall tire mileage and fuel efficiency both increase ("the lemons are squeezed better"), and sustainability performance increases.

A reduction in fuel consumption of just 2.5 km per 100 km represents annual savings of €3,200 for a long-haul transport travelling over 120,000 km—reductions of at least 2.1% in total cost of ownership and 8 tonnes in CO_2 emissions.[4] There is more: With this usage-based model, Michelin has a vested interest in making its tires as long-lasting as possible ("growing juicier lemons"), as more kilometers now equates to more revenues. This aligns the firm's interest with those of the customers and of the planet. Last, Michelin needs to think more deeply about how it could increase its tires' recyclability, as all tires are eventually returned to their owner: the firm.

These examples show how filling the "knowledge gap"—the difference between the optimal use of an offering and the typical use of it—fosters efficiency gains and, thus, Resonance. XaaS models like those of Rolls Royce and Michelin are one way of doing this, but they are not the only way.

Another way to close the knowledge gap is by *deskilling* the use of the product to make it more resilient, robust—or intelligent. Nest thermostats learn from users' behavior. If users regularly turn the heating down at certain times of day, they incorporate this practice into the weekly heating schedule. They also access householders' cell phone data to determine where they are. If they are away from home, they turn down the heat or reduce the air-conditioning.

Alternatively, firms can *teach* users how to maximize their offerings. Chemical major BASF has launched its GrowSmart University, a content hub that offers farmers videos, e-books, and other media to help them maximize yields from their crops. In this case, the firm has gone to great lengths to increase the capability of its customers: It has become an educator.

Whether through XaaS, deskilling, or teaching, reducing misuse offers a clear route to Usage Resonance through efficiency gains.

UNDERUSE. Products commonly lie idle. Customers might be unaware of how rarely they use the things they buy. Yet their ignorance hides an awkward truth: Much of what is made is left to rot. We noted earlier how little of its life a car spends rolling on the road. We noted that occasionwear—particularly ladieswear—is often worn just a few times before it goes out of fashion and becomes unappealing to its owner. Now consider that power-tool manufacturer Hilti France calculated that drills for the DIY market make an average four holes per year.

We are all prone to chronic underutilization in our daily lives. After all, how many of us utilize more than 5% of Microsoft Excel's capabilities?

Sometimes, third-party firms can capture value from the underuse of products. Consider the market for construction equipment rental. Business and householders in most cities across the world can hire jack-hammers, breakers, and floor sanders. This allows the customer to save money otherwise spent on buying a tool that they would rarely use—and would have to store while idle.

Rent the Runway is a fashion rental subscription service in the United States. It allows its customers to borrow designer clothes for a period, then exchange them for different pieces. Its average customer borrows $34,000 worth of clothing for an annual subscription of approximately $1,200 per year. That is a resonant package: The customer extracts nearly 30 times the value from her subscription.[5]

And the clothing—typically high-value, well-made, designer ladieswear—is being put to great use. Dresses are circulated among many Rent the Runway clients weekly, rather than gathering dust in the wardrobe of just one woman, before going out of fashion. It is the opposite of throwaway "fast fashion," where each dress is worn just a few times then discarded. The Rent the Runway model extracts maximal "juice" from each dress. The model incentivizes the manufacture and supply of well-made, durable clothing, rather than cheap womenswear that cannot be worn more than a few times.

LINEAR-ONLY ABUSE. Let's talk about waste. According to Circle Economy, only about 7% of the materials we use are cycled back to the economy after their use.[6] And, if anything, this number has been going down recently. The remainder stick to the flawed model of take-make-waste—waste is a cost of doing business that someone, somewhere, must pay.

As we said in chapter 2, an industrial process has two outputs—its product or service and the superfluous material it produces. This superfluous material is deemed to be waste. Yet there is no such thing as waste—just material that is in the wrong place. Throwing that material away is an abuse of resources.

This thinking is at the heart of one alternative to take-make-waste: the *reuse* model. There are several exemplars of this. One example is Brambles—a "reverse logistics" firm that makes money from materials that are in the wrong place. Reverse logistics means removing items from (rather than delivering to) customers. Brambles says its circular reuse model typically reduces its customers waste by 66%.[7] It helps customers recycle unused materials such as wood, food, and plastics. For example, it used the empty leg of Walmart Canada truck journeys to transport empty wooden racks from the retail giant's gardening departments to recycling facilities. The project salvaged 2,000 metric tonnes of waste wood—which was reclaimed for biofuel, sawdust, and bedding for farm animals.

In further proof that one man's waste is another man's resource, Neste, the sustainable fuels and renewable feedstock manufacturer, utilizes cooking oil previously used in McDonald's fast-food outlets.[8]

Some reuse models remain in-house. Carmaker BMW deconstructs its own cars at the end of their lives—salvaging materials for its next round of manufacture. Its new cars are comprised of up to 30% recycled and reused materials. TCL does so similarly with its cell phones.

For some companies, *resale* (rather than reuse) is the prime model. Apple reconditions and resells its cell phones on a grand scale. The brand alone accounts for half of the total market for refurbished phones globally.[9]

The downside

Despite their multiple advantages, the models have many downsides. There remain several reasons for consumers to avoid a shift to XaaS models.

The first reason is *inertia*. Consumers can be slow to change their behavior. Furthermore, it takes time and effort for firms to update their processes and organization to enable sharing service models. Implementation is difficult. There is a long—and steep—learning curve. Developmental costs can be high. Crucially, firms must be sure that the new business model is more profitable than the traditional business model they are currently using.

The second reason is the continuing *lure of ownership* for many customers. Porsche Drive is a Cars as a Service (CaaS) offering under which customers—like Isabelle in the chapter introduction—can flip one model for another at short notice. This might seem like perfection for performance-car enthusiasts, few of whom would decline the opportunity to flit throughout Porsche's wide range of models. Yet many Porsche Drive customers still end up buying a Porsche. The service acts as a taster for driving the vehicles and—in many cases—users fall in love with a model and want to own it.

The third reason in the case of sharing usage models is *availability anxiety.* This involves a situation where customers worry that they might need a particular product at a particular time at a particular location. They fear that service models might fail to deliver this and—thus—the only way to assure permanent availability is to own a product and store it locally. This is why many householders own expensive power tools that they use just a handful of times per year: When they need the tool, they can be sure it is on hand, rather than stored in a remote location and potentially unavailable.

The ugly truth

These customer downsides are not the only reason firms are reluctant to switch. Many avoid moving to sharing service models, even though they can benefit customers and the planet. The reality is that many firms cite the downsides to mask the ugly truth: *They are concerned that greater efficiency will diminish their profits.*

How can this be? There are several ways. First, *decreasing misuse* can prompt sales decreases for the product and associated consumables.

Consider, for example, how the misuse of a printing machine would likely cause greater ink consumption and increase the frequency of servicing. Were misuse reduced, the printing-machine firm would sell less ink and provide fewer technician service appointments.

Similarly, *decreasing overuse* can also trigger lower sales volumes. A toothpaste manufacturer discovered that by widening the diameter of the toothpaste tube, customers wasted more paste and—thus—bought more tubes. Deliberate wastefulness caused higher consumption.

Now think about *decreasing underuse.* This too can diminish product sales. Imagine the potential impact on drill sales if householders switched en masse to renting power tools only when they needed them!

Finally, *increasing reuse* can weaken product sales. For example, the more consumers who buy used phones, the fewer who demand new ones.

The race to Usage Resonance

Resonators are aware of the potential pitfalls of the big shift to usage business models, but resolve to go around them.

This is because those with a true Resonator mindset always prioritize the value-add for their customers. They understand that the explosion of digital technology can and will make service models ever more viable, and so Resonant firms think, "if we fail to shift, someone else will." To Resonators, moving to service models is not a question of "whether." It is a question of "when" and "how."

Achieving Usage Resonance

As we explored earlier, by focusing on reducing customer usage inefficiencies, Usage Resonance is inherently virtuous for the planet. The key to making these models work is to solve the conundrum at its heart:

TABLE 4-1

Making Usage Resonance work

	Customers	Firms
Driver	Increase incentive to purchase	Increase financial value
Conditions	Criticality	Scalability
	Reversibility	Complexity
	Transparency	Compatibility

How do we enhance customer-value while simultaneously becoming more profitable? As we have seen, creating efficiency gains by reducing misuse, underuse, and overuse and increasing reuse can present barriers to profit. The key is to learn to overcome these barriers.

The starting point for all prospective Usage Resonators is to analyze the initial situation. Thereafter, they must manage it to ensure they benefit themselves and their customers. Here, we show how.

For effective analysis, we always consider both sides of the trade. For a model to be resonant, both the firm and the customer need one critical *driver.* Furthermore, they must both fulfil three important *conditions* (see table 4-1).

Let us begin with exploring the customer side of the trade.

The Customer Side

The critical driver for customers is that we increase their incentive to purchase vis-à-vis the current offer. Figure 4-1 plots the offer's current situation along their traditional benefits and price.

Any offer that is above the black (value) line would be unattractive, as it lowers the incentive to purchase. For example, moving the offer to point A would mean the benefits are marginally improved for a steep

FIGURE 4-1

Current offer versus traditional benefits

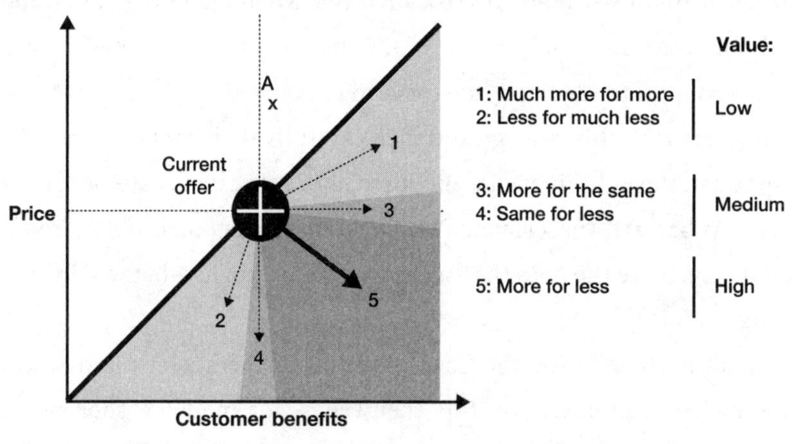

price increase, which is an unappealing offer—"more (benefits) for much more (price)." Attractive offers will be situated below the value line; but where? As shown in figure 4-1, there are five overarching approaches to do this, and we will briefly introduce each of them by increasing order of attractiveness.

Zones 1 and 2 are unlikely to gain significant traction from the customer's perspective. Zone 1, offering *much more for more*, could be appealing in theory; however, it will be challenging to persuade customers to pay a higher price given the uncertainty and magnitude of change involved. Zone 2, offering *less for much less*, could be effective, especially for companies seeking to reduce their cost structures. Nevertheless, it may encounter resistance from parts of the organization, for which providing less is viewed as a regressive step.

Zones 3 and 4 are appealing. Offering *more for the same* can work, but customers may still be doubtful about the actual benefits. Zone 4's proposition of *the same for less* is more attractive as it offers cost savings, a constant customer interest.

However, in our experience, firms should really strive to go to zone 5, offering *more for less*. Recall the customer inertia that we mentioned earlier; think also about the risk involved when changing "anything" both for consumers and organizations. The way to go is to make a generous proposal that will be "too good to pass."

So, start with this strategy and then carefully monitor how customers respond to the uplift in value, and learn about revealed customer preferences. What are the elements of value that customers feel strongly about? What are the ones that are not as important as what was initially thought?

Recall Porsche Drive, the CaaS model from the luxury German carmaker where customers can "flip" their vehicle for another at short notice. The initial offering allowed unlimited flips—24 hours a day, seven days a week. A very generous offer. When a customer called for a new vehicle on her app, a concierge would arrive to deliver her new choice, then drive the car she had previously back to the garage. Porsche then progressively learned about customer preferences and successively reduced the flipping period first to weekdays and then to eight hours per day during weekdays, but customers did not really object to these restrictions.

It learned that, during the first few weeks, customers were prone to frequent flipping. They enjoyed the experience of trying numerous models. They relished the opportunity to test-drive them. Yet, after a short while, the frequency plummeted, and the restriction from 24/7 to 8/5 was not perceived as a great loss for the majority of drivers. Customers soon learned their preferences. The appeal of changing a car they loved for another wore off. While Porsche's concierge service is excellent, there are still some transaction costs for the customer. She must find a suitable window in which to make the exchange, then wait for the concierge to arrive—which precluded her driving the car or making other appointments.

We call this phenomenon the *Nespresso Effect*. Customer data reveals that new Nespresso users typically begin with a large variety of pods, sometimes trying the whole line of 24 coffees. However, following a short period using the service, this typically falls to as few as three choices. Customers realize their own preferences and choose, say, one decaffeinated variety, one long, and one short.

With Porsche, the reduction is often even more profound: The flipping could cease entirely. Rather, as we have seen, many Drive customers learn their own preferences to such a degree that they settle on just one model and—having grown fond of the Porsche experience—buy the car outright.

Even with the reductions to the service made by Porsche, customers continue to gain value from the carmaker's model. With any service model, firms must demonstrate the efficiency and sustainability gains for customers. Three key questions help firms do this.

- Does the offering decrease the customer's total cost of ownership?
- Does the offering reduce other costs?
- Does the offering increase business and/or sustainability value for customers (or customers' customers)?

Let's address each in turn by exploring Hilti's Tools as a Service models and the TaaS model offered by Michelin. Both models decrease the customer's total cost of ownership. Michelin's model offers a lower cost per mile than buying tires. Hilti's model means customers get the optimal selection of tools delivered to on-site for a particular job. This lowers administration costs compared to customers buying the tools and moving them to the right site.

Both models also reduce other costs. Hilti reduces the costs of manpower. Its tools are tracked. And when they are damaged, there is less downtime spent on replacing them. By optimizing the choice of tires, Michelin typically delivers a 2% reduction in fuel costs for trucks using the service, and corresponding CO_2 emission savings.

Furthermore, Hilti and Michelin increase value for customers—and customers' customers. Hilti's model makes it easier for customers to meet construction deadlines. In addition, they show that the client company is a serious player that uses premium tools. Similarly, Michelin-served trucking companies are less likely to have delivery problems. This improves their reputation as reliable logistics providers.

Firms should systematically quantify and monetize elements of value, including sustainability benefits. They can use classic tools like word equations and interactive spreadsheets. Advanced firms, such as Atlas Copco, have created sophisticated CO_2 calculators. Firms should note that customers' internal costs are hard to assess, often poorly documented and underestimated, and sometimes misclassified as "fixed." The key here is to address these challenges and ensure a compelling value proposition before actively marketing the new service model.

Conditions

Now let's explore the three important conditions. The first condition is *criticality*. To make a success of XaaS, the offering must fall into the sweet spot that exists between "not worth it" and "too critical."

Shifting involves changing the organization and its process. Thus, customers will be unwilling to switch to a service model if the gains are insufficiently substantial. This is further proof that firms must ensure that customers understand the value of shifting—and are aware of the full costs of retaining a traditional model. Ahrend offered Furniture as a Service (FaaS). It demonstrated that firms could save 2% on furniture costs by renting the furniture rather than buying it. That saving *included* the hidden costs of owning furniture, such as storage and servicing.[10] The gains are modest, and arguably "not worth it." Thus, its FaaS model has been rather unsuccessful.

At the other end of the scale, customers can deem a function "too critical" to outsource. In such scenarios, firms must convince customers that the service they provide is now the industry standard—such that the function customers are being asked to outsource can no longer be considered a source of competitive advantage. It is fascinating to consider how this has changed for Michelin's customers over time. When trucking fleets were "transportation firms," the fleet's tires were an important cost center that companies were wary of outsourcing to a subscription model. Today, those firms have transmogrified into "logistics operators"—with warehousing, IT, and communications infrastructure. Thus, tires are a less important slice of the operation—generating an opening for TaaS.

The second important condition for success is *reversibility*. Customers will be unwilling to subscribe to service models if they consider them a one-way door. Rather, they must be reassured that they can exit contracts when it suits them. In some cases, it is easy to do this. HP's Instant Ink model delivers paper and ink to customers using digital technology to monitor usage. It allows customers to cancel at any time and pay only up until the last day of the billing month.

In cases where the value and gains only materialize when the customer organization has changed, the challenge is greater. The benefits of Michelin's tires service only fully materialize when the customers realize maintenance savings, which take time to manifest. In such cases, firms must hold customers' hands—and outline how the gains will materialize in due course. Interestingly, having competition here on these business models can play a positive role. Customers are more likely to shift if they know that they could change providers if the service is not on a par with that promised.

The final condition is *transparency*. Ensure that customers grasp how the firm can offer more for less. Failing to do so will prompt customer suspicion—either with the new offering ("What's the catch?"), or with the current one ("Why so generous now? Where were they cheating us?"). Firms can eradicate this suspicion by ensuring they have at least one compelling "financial value driver." We explore such drivers in the next section.

The Firm Side

The critical driver for firms is to *increase financial value*. How can firms make more money, while being more generous with customers and delivering sustainability benefits? Sure, there are the classic benefits of selling services: Services increase sales, they offer greater profits, and they recur, which potentially creates a sticky relationship with your customers.[11] Yet firms should avoid overestimating these benefits when developing Usage Resonance because they are often insufficient for business success.[12]

First, it is all too easy to *overestimate gains in market share* that firms will derive from the shift to a resonant XaaS model. Gaining any share at all is uncertain. Third parties who are currently providing the service will fight back. And, if your service removes work from internal parties—such as tire-maintenance employees in our Michelin example—your service will render some people redundant. This will be unpopular with staff and generate resistance.

Second, *profitability is hard to calculate* because the total costs of delivering services are tricky to quantify. The mindset changes to deliver these services are important, from maximizing to optimizing productivity (to make sure that the service levels are on par with the customers' expectations). The risk is that they expend too much time and money overservicing unprofitable elements of a service account, for example on long calls with clients to discuss problems with deliveries that would have been avoided had the process been sufficiently robust. In any case, firms must be wary of the so-called Valley of Death—the likely fall in profits in the early stage of a shift to a service model. Gains likely arrive later—but the launch phase can be arduous. It can lead to proponents of the service model coming under internal pressure as the firm waits—impatiently—for profits to manifest.

Third, firms risk *overplaying the relational value* born of shifting to a recurring service. XaaS does offer a door to more intimacy with customers. Yet companies must have a clear plan to capture this potential value. Even if a plan exists, they must be wary of overestimating the gains from it. A service model remains a sales transaction—it should not be confused with a love affair.

To overcome these obstacles to success, firms need at least one clear and compelling *financial value driver* (FVD). Recall our lemon example: These critical drivers are ways to squeeze the fruit further—to extract more juice from the same product. Some of these FVDs depend on the use model. Let's explore those further.

Misuse (and overuse)

How would the performance of the product or asset improve if the firm owned, operated, and maintained it? Modest differences are insufficient for success. To qualify as an FVD, the change in performance must be sizable.

Recall, for example, Rolls Royce's EaaS. Guajardo et al. compared the performance of EaaS to the performance of traditional models, using Mean Time Between Unscheduled Removals (MTBUR) as a key metric; they discovered that MTBUR increased 25–40% compared to traditional models whereby customers bought and maintained the engines.[13]

A similarly substantial change can be witnessed with Michelin's TaaS. The manufacturer promotes its 4 Lives policy, which regrooves and remixes tires to refresh them and save money for its customers. By furnishing customers with its own expertise, the new model enables more tires to complete all four lives. This reduces total cost for customers from €2 to €1.3 per 1,000 km.[14]

Underuse

What is the current usage level of the product? How many times is it used and/or for how long? To qualify as an FVD, there must be a multiplier effect—that is, a fivefold increase in usage rather than a 5% increase. Recall Rent the Runway—the Clothing as a Service brand. Data reveals that many clothes that are purchased are worn very few times—if at all. In the United Kingdom, for example, some 8% of purchased clothes are *never* worn. The underuse problem is more profound in occasionwear, particularly women's occasionwear. These outfits, typically purchased for social events such as weddings or black-tie dinners, are often worn only a few times before they fall out of fashion or the owner tires of being seen in them. Under Rent the Runway's model, each designer dress gets many wears—as several women in disparate locations and social groups borrow the dresses over each season.

A similar multiplier is found in Tools as a Service. Recall that when drills are owned, they make an average four holes per year. Yet when loaned, they need just two people per month to make four holes to average almost *100 holes* per year, a 25x multiplier.

Reuse

What is the economic value of the reuse (partial or total) or resale? This must be more than just a sustainability undertaking. To qualify as an FVD there should—or could—be substantial intrinsic value in the product at the end of its life. This value must be a cold, hard economic calculation of value—independent of the sustainability saving realized by reusing it.

Consider Apple iPhones. Used units of earlier generations command great economic value and, when reconditioned, can achieve premium prices. Palm Group makes money from recycling paper into corrugated board. The resale value of the paper is modest. Yet the recycling process generates sufficient volumes to allow Palm to use Valmet pulping machines, which are highly efficient. Thus, reuse has conferred economies of scale that Palm profits from.

Yet when reuse fails, it fails badly. Textiles recycling firm Renewcell claimed to "make fashion circular" by creating new clothes from old cloth. It had a great plant and great buzz. It won multiple sustainability prizes. Yet the hard economics were lacking. The company filed for bankruptcy in 2024.[15]

Multiple drivers

Some FVDs are independent of specific business models. For example, Rent the Runway extracts value by maximizing economies of scale. These economies are born of its formidable buying power—and its prestigious profile. It pays wholesale prices for its stock, not retail prices. And it is possible to imagine that sometimes it pays nothing for new designer dresses. This is because these designers gain substantial promotional value by featuring in its portfolio.

In other cases, firms use FVDs in combination. For example, Porsche Drive has two FVDs. It takes advantage of underuse by loaning cars that would otherwise lie idle. It benefits from reuse by selling vehicles that were previously loaned. Similarly, Rent the Runway benefits from multiple FVDs: the underuse of designer fashions *and* its economies of scale.

Conditions

Just as with customers, firms must meet three conditions to achieve Usage Resonance.

The first condition is *scalability.* The additional market opportunity must be correctly assessed. Is the likely growth 5x or +5%? This scalability depends on the intensity of maintenance and operations. The opportunity also depends on the relative importance of consumables versus the product itself—that is, the classic razor versus blades equation.

Industrial digital printers have sales of $250,000–$1,000,000 per year, with margins of probably around 10%. It is the *sales of the ink* that make the difference. Its ink sales of $100,000–$150,000 per year can command a 50% margin.

The second important condition is *complexity.* Can the firm keep complexity at a manageable level? This complexity can be dissected in three parts. One is *structural complexity.* For each customer, how many touchpoints are there likely to be? Which skills and capabilities must be deployed? And over how many geographies? For example, BOBST or Valmet are complex machines that demand significant skills and capabilities to run them. Michelin and Rolls Royce must move their assets across geographies to deliver their respective TaaS and EaaS models. Caterpillar must be able to access mines in remote locations to deliver its Elevators as a Service offering. The greater a firm's structural complexity, the more challenging it will be to execute a service model.

Another type of complexity to consider is *transfer complexity.* To what extent can firms transfer knowledge gained from one customer to benefit another? How much do the needs of each customer—or each industry—differ? For example, Lenovo serves many verticals. But its customers are more homogenous than Securitas, which offers Security as a Service (SaaS) to customers as disparate as nuclear plants, semiconductor plants, refineries, and high net-worth condominiums. The more heterogeneous a firms' customers, the harder it will be to support a service model.

The final type of complexity is *supply chain complexity.* Does the firm rely on a third-party or parties to deliver the service? For example,

Michelin and Caterpillar use dealers to sell their services that are not employed directly. Using third-party suppliers adds a level of complexity that firms must be able to manage.

The final condition that must be met is *compatibility.* This is a question of culture. Firms must consider honestly whether the development of a XaaS model will fit the philosophy of the company. Does the firm have a culture of exploration or exploitation? A good way to frame this question is to see which of these profiles best fits your firm. Is it profile A: exploration, risk-taking, initiative-driven, test & learn, and ask-for-forgiveness? Or is it profile B: exploitation, risk-averse, process-driven, make-it-perfect, and ask-for-permission? If it's the latter, the shift might be difficult to enact. Yet if it's the former, colleagues are likely to be open to the opportunity. Consider sportswear major Decathlon. The French retailer pledges: "At Decathlon, we minimize hierarchical structures to enable entrepreneurship at all levels."[16] Thus, the company seniors were open to the concept of a sports equipment rental model.

Professional Lemon Squeezing

Let's go back to the lemon example we used at the start of this chapter. The difference between customers and firms was startling. Customers' usage of lemons can be quite inefficient only a small portion of juice can be extracted, and most of the lemon is wasted. When firms take charge, they can significantly change the process, from the lemon selection to the squeezing process to the reuse of pulp, skin, and seeds.

Usage Resonance consists in doing just that: shifting the process from customers to firms. The gains are significant, both in terms of business efficiency and sustainability performance, and both are perfectly correlated. As in Product Resonance, sustainability gains can be made optional for Grays. And in the end, all customers—Grays, Blues and Greens—are better off.

The question is no longer "whether," but "when" and "how." These two last questions are obviously linked, and this chapter focused on helping crystallize this difficult endeavor: making attractive offers to customers, while being more profitable than traditional business models.

This is a significant change. While Product Resonance needs little from customers, Usage Resonance demands that consumers modify habits and organizations adjust processes. This starts from the job title of "purchasing manager," which may evolve into "usage manager." Usage Resonance is also made possible by the development of digital technology; we will devote chapter 6 to this key enabler.

5

Strategic Resonance

Using Sustainability to Grow into New Playing Fields

Stephanie, a Paris-based entrepreneur providing organic meals to top firms, needs more delivery vehicles due to business growth. She seeks help from Bill, her friend and fellow entrepreneur.

"Which car manufacturer should I consider?" she asks. "Volkswagen, Renault, or perhaps Toyota?" Bill replies, "Actually, I suggest looking into Michelin. Their Watéa light electric vehicle offering is great." Stephanie responds, "What? Is Michelin now competing with car manufacturers?"

Strategy centers on two fundamental questions—where to play, and how to win.[1]

The first two paths of Resonance—Product Resonance and Usage Resonance—addressed the question of how to win. And all the examples we used were from firms creating Resonance in their "current playing fields." But the question of where to play is not just about competing in a firm's current playing fields, but about exploring new ones as well.

Firms have always grappled with the question of whether to move into new playing fields based on their competitive strengths and potential advantages. Yet the idea of using sustainability as the passport to strengthen a firm's strategy by expanding into adjacent playing fields is a novel approach. We call this *Strategic Resonance.*

Firms can go into new playing fields because they notice that customers or complementors are struggling with a problem that results in unwanted outputs. In figure 2-2, inefficiencies and externalities of other firms make it possible for a firm to explore new "where to play" adjacencies.

Let's look at the example of Grundfos, a leader in intelligent water pumps. The firm's intelligent products are used in heating systems. They provide building owners (the customers) the desired temperature, while delivering up to 80% savings on electrical pump usage.[2] But customer needs often extend beyond Grundfos's products because building owners care about overall energy costs. Serving this overall energy efficiency need would require a firm to look more broadly at complementors' products in its own value chain (e.g., maintenance firms, controllers), but also at others' products that are serving this need (e.g., lighting, appliances). Of course, a firm cannot and should not try to do everything; it is a matter of strategic choice on "where to play."

Strategic Resonance: Expanding into Adjacent Playing Fields

There are two primary adjacencies any firm can pursue—products and markets.[3] A product adjacency is where a firm introduces new products within its markets (or current playing fields) to solve broader customer needs. A market adjacency is where a firm goes into new playing fields with its current products. A firm can do both as well—introducing new products and going into new markets. Let's look at how firms are using sustainability to pursue these adjacencies.

Volvo and Nio: Product adjacency

Consider electric vehicle (EV) carmakers such as Volvo and Nio. Volvo, which made a very strong commitment to mainly sell EV cars, realized that the energy used to charge the battery was often from non-green sources. This could raise customer skepticism about Volvo's true commitment to sustainability. To alleviate this customer concern, Volvo decided to introduce green energy products to serve EV buyers. It did so via a partnership with Iberdrola, a utility company in Spain. Under the partnership, Iberdrola installs public charging stations at Volvo dealerships. These stations are powered by 100% certified green energy. Additionally, Iberdrola offers a green energy-based home charging solution to Volvo customers.[4]

Nio, a Chinese EV car maker, took a different approach. Nio positions itself as a lifestyle company, which delivers an exceptional EV car ownership experience. The company discovered that range anxiety and battery longevity are a barrier to the purchase of its EVs. To make both concerns a non-issue for purchase, Nio offers a battery-swapping subscription service.[5] The battery subscription service allows customers to swap their battery in three minutes, while waiting in their car at Nio's swapping stations. The company owns and operates about 3,445 stations and is also connected to almost 1.9 million third-party chargers. The company completed over 73 million battery swaps as of June 2025.[6] In the first half of 2025, NIO Inc. delivered 114,150 vehicles in total, marking a year-over-year increase of 30.6%.[7]

Lysol and Ford: Market adjacency

Lysol has traditionally been positioned in the consumer market as a surface sanitizer. Inspired by UN Sustainable Development Goal (SDG) #3—"to ensure healthy lives and promote well-being for all at all ages"—the Lysol team reconceptualized its brand purpose as follows: "Keep your loved ones illness-free."[8] Since children are more prone to illnesses,

Lysol's marketing team asked themselves a simple question—how do we keep loved ones illness-free in schools? This led to Lysol launching the Healthy Habits in Schools program with the mission of "fighting the spread of preventable illnesses."[9]

The Lysol example is one of a market adjacency—expanding from the consumer market into a B2B arrangement with the school market—with mostly similar products. The impetus for going into this adjacency was triggered by a customer problem—schools are a hotbed for spreading illnesses among children. This led to absenteeism, an unwanted output. Absenteeism impacts not only the progress of children, but school funding as well. This is because a portion of a school's funding is tied to the number of days kids attend the school.

Ford's F-150 Lightning has a simple message of performance and affordability—it delivers performance by accelerating from 0 to 60 mph in four seconds, it excels in moving heavy loads, and it provides money savings of about $11,000 in three years.[10] But that's not all. With the tagline of "Life, Electrified," it promises to "Power your life from tools to tailgates."[11] The Ford F-150 Pro Power Onboard powers a circular saw to run for over 44 hours, or a campsite for up to three weeks.[12]

Ford has not stopped here. It co-created with Sunrun a system to extend this value into a new playing field—the home. Ford's Charge Station Pro and Home Integration System works seamlessly between a home and truck. In the event of a home electrical outage, the F-150 powers the home with the equivalent storage of 10 home batteries.[13] The homeowner can run the home as normal, including all appliances. The Home Integration System can also be paired with solar. Homeowners get easy invoicing—they pay just one monthly rate.[14]

Siemens: Product and market adjacency

Siemens is one of the world's industrial powerhouses, with a revenue of €75.9 billion in 2024. The firm has a diverse portfolio that spans a breadth of sectors, including industrial automation, intelligent building infrastructure, sustainable energy systems, advanced drive technology, and healthcare.

Within Siemens, the Energy and Sustainability Services (ESS) business area has a charter to support customers in decarbonization and energy cost reduction. There was a notable collaboration between ESS and Heineken, one of the world's premier brewing companies, to spearhead an ambitious energy optimization initiative.[15] The partnership materialized through a strategically crafted multi-phase program designed to reduce energy use and carbon emissions.

Initially, Siemens leaned on its established expertise in building infrastructure optimization. Think of these services as energy optimization on the periphery of a customer's operations. This included lighting systems, air handling units, and HVAC systems. At one time, Siemen's engineers used to walk each building site and perform energy audits. Back then, they provided "fix-and-leave" services.

But as customers, such as Heineken, began asking for *continuous* decarbonization support, rather than onetime fixes, Siemens began adapting its approach. Its AI tools, for example, cut the time to do energy audits from one year to one month and slash cost by a factor of ten without losing audit quality.

Heineken presented Siemens with a complex challenge: to optimize the energy-intensive core of their brewing operations. For ESS, this was a pivotal shift from traditional building management to involvement in a client's production processes. Siemens had to develop an intimate understanding of Heineken's brewing operations, effectively moving from the "outer shell" of facility management to the very heart of the production floor.

Heineken challenged ESS to optimize its de-alcoholization process, which is an energy-intensive step of removing alcohol from beer. Typically, Siemens would have performed an energy audit and created a PDF document of what needed to be improved. But Siemens turned the energy audit report from a PDF into a living asset. What does this mean?

Siemens created a digital twin of the de-alcoholization process. A digital twin is quite simply a living or identical replica that mimics a process. The digital twin allowed Siemens to collect real-time data about the de-alcoholization process and run simulations to see how it could be optimized. Simulations using the digital twin identified that about 70% of energy consumption was linked to the heating and cooling processes during the brewing procedure. By recycling wasted heat from a cooling process, ESS was able to deliver significant cost savings for Heineken, while also reducing emissions by 20% to 40%. Siemens is now scaling the solution to fifteen Heineken breweries with the goal of significant energy savings and 50% CO_2 reduction by 2025.[16]

Siemens' strategic expansion beyond traditional building services has increased profit margins, while delivering positive environmental impact to customers. This evolution from peripheral building solutions to comprehensive operational integration has helped customers avoid approximately 144 million metric tons of CO_2 emissions through products and solutions.

Watèa by Michelin: Product and market adjacency

France is at the forefront of decarbonizing mobility. The country has Low Emission Zones in urban areas. Vehicles must display a sticker that indicates their emission category. Vehicles with the high carbon-emissions sticker are prohibited from entering certain zones. And, in the coming years, the country plans to expand these zones and make emission targets even more stringent.[17]

Now, imagine you are a small business. Buying new EVs entails a capital investment and uncertain return on investment. Michelin recognized the opportunity to help small and medium-sized enterprises

(SMEs)—such as last-mile delivery subcontractors, craftsmen, and construction workers—manage an expensive energy transition.

Traditionally, Michelin's B2B transactions involved selling tires to fleet owners. In 2021, the company entered the electric mobility space. This segment was an adjacency. Yet it is consistent with its purpose of "giving people a better way of moving forward."[18] The company introduced a new subscription-based business offering called Watèa. The subscription service offers SMEs electric or hydrogen vehicles and charging solutions.[19] The end-to-end solution enables SMEs to lower capital investment and operate their business "as usual," while meeting regulatory requirements. Watéa also enables its customers to identify the best routes for charging—a solution that saves SMEs valuable business time.[20]

When to Consider Strategic Resonance?

Let's look at a few principles that help a firm decide whether and how it might move into an adjacent space using sustainability as the driving or facilitating factor.

- **Does going into an adjacency protect your core resonance value proposition?** Imagine your firm offers a value proposition that leverages sustainability. Now consider EV cars. You make a case that the annual fuel and maintenance costs of an EV are significantly lower than conventional vehicles.[21] This is your core value proposition. All good, right? Sadly, no. A sustainability-conscious customer might question whether the power source to *charge* the vehicle is sustainable. Should you be unable to prove it, they might sneer at you.

  This is an opportunity for a firm to protect the core and extend its value proposition by exploring adjacencies. This is what we saw Volvo do earlier in this chapter. Recall that the Swedish carmaker formed a partnership with Iberdrola.

Nio took a different approach. It wanted to improve the EV experience for customers, by making EVs more affordable and convenient. Nio entered the adjacency of battery swapping, a heavy-duty service business. It reduced Total Cost of Ownership by making battery purchase optional. And, while on the road, customers could simply swap the battery in under three minutes if it required recharging.

The idea here is simple—you have a core value proposition that is embedded in sustainability. Yet this core can be questioned. You expand to an adjacent market or offering with a sustainability lens to make your core value proposition stronger.

- **Does going into an adjacency meet the true job-to-be-done and improve competitive positioning?** Too often firms focus on the "job" that their own products do for a customer. For example, a diaper maker that uses excellent dryness materials may consider "better sleep" (for both baby and parents) as an outcome of dryness. Think of this as the "product" job-to-be-done (JTBD). It is no doubt important.

  But if you ask parents about the true job to be done, they will often speak about baby development. It does not mean a firm has to tackle baby development, but this is a choice a firm must make. One important criterion to consider is whether going into an adjacency is doable, attractive, and improves a firm's competitive positioning. Let's look at an example.

  Mahindra Group, an Indian conglomerate with revenues of $16.44 billion in 2023–2024, exemplifies Adjacency Resonance.[22] Its Agri division had a strong presence in agricultural equipment. For decades, it focused on becoming the market leader in this space. Its chairman, Anand Mahindra, reimagined the purpose of this division. He saw that many small firms could not afford their equipment. These farmers were poor—and were engaging in farm practices that were both inefficient and environmentally harmful.

Was there no way of helping them? The Agri division reimagined its vision and business to focus on building "a nation of champion farmers." By way of achieving its vision, the firm introduced Krish-e in October 2020, with the goal of radically increasing the yield and income of struggling farmers, which is the farmer's true JTBD.

Krish-e started providing equipment loans to make tillers, sprayers, and harvesters more affordable to farmers. It also offers advisory, digital, and precision-farming services, including facilitation of onsite operations.[23] These services strengthen the relationship with farmers, while also growing the core equipment business.

Mahindra educates farmers on new ways of growing crops to obtain better yields, thereby alleviating poverty. The division's agronomic specialists persuade farmers to experiment with modern ways of growing crops on small plots of land. Today, it has more than 13,000 "Takneek plots"—single-acre plots demonstrating better ways of farming. "This is giving us a lot of heart," says Ramesh Ramachandran, senior vice president at Mahindra's farm equipment business. "We are out there on the field. This is a free service for farmers and our engagement with them is very simple. Help us improve your income per acre, just work with us and let us hold your hand."[24]

Krish-e is showing promise—both for Mahindra and for farmers. By 2022, Krish-e had engaged two million farmers, generating gross merchandise value of US$40 million for Mahindra. It aims to increase that to US$200 million by 2025.[25]

- **Do you have a "right to play" in an adjacency?** Going into an adjacency always brings up the "right to play" question. Will your customers see you as a credible provider of products in the new adjacency? Can you build the right competencies?

Market adjacencies with current products (or slightly modified products) tend to be easier from the aspect of building credibility with customers. This is especially the case if a firm has a known brand. Lysol's entry into schools or serving other B2B markets (e.g., airlines) to arrest the spread of preventable illnesses would make sense to customers. They would see it as a logical adjacency.

Firms that own shipping lines (i.e., ocean transportation) and ports have expanded into end-to-end logistics. This move is partially driven by an intent to address a key frustration of cargo owners, which is overpayment for logistics services because of massive inefficiencies in a highly fragmented supply chain. These inefficiencies existed because many small players used archaic and inefficient processes to perform tasks that include customs clearance, storage, and local transportation.

Firms that have made the shift to offer end-to-end logistics services have had mixed success for several reasons. It is not easy to modernize archaic supply chains that are major contributors to greenhouse gas emissions. It takes sophisticated information systems to tracks good and do efficient routing. Without such systems, both customer value and sustainability gains will be minimal. Many of these firms lack such systems and have had long and difficult journeys to build them from scratch.

Just as complicated is the fact that parties these firms considered as collaborators become competitors. For a shipping firm that offers end-to-end logistics services, a terminal (port) operator is a collaborator in the value chain. If the terminal operator decides to offer the same end-to-end services, they essentially become competitors and collaborators. This requires the ability to manage complex relationships.

Resonance and Competitiveness

The question of competition often comes up in our discussion with firms. But, not just in consideration of adjacency moves as described above. The primary strategy question that comes up is whether a firm can compete on sustainability. Can firms genuinely monetize it?

This question is not related to Strategy Resonance only, but is also equally pertinent to firms pursuing Product Resonance and Usage Resonance. So, as we conclude Part One of the book, we'll turn to a general discussion of whether and how firms can make money from sustainability.

Sustainability: Monetization tests

One of our clients provides milking equipment to the dairy industry. They had diligently studied the sustainability commitments of a dairy customer, and their strategy document spoke extensively about sustainability and about partnering with suppliers who would help them meet their commitments. They prepared a presentation demonstrating that they could help the dairy customer with their Scope 1 greenhouse gas (GHG) emissions, and that they were better than competitors. Our client felt everything had stacked up to finally pay for its sustainability efforts.

Forget about getting paid. The customer, to whom the presentation was made, showed little interest in the sustainability value proposition. Why? It transpired that the dairy customer was working with its animal feed and supplements suppliers to meet its emissions-reduction goals. This made sense because cows—not dairy farm equipment—were the prime source of its greenhouse gas emissions. Thus, our client's efficient milking apparatus would help only marginally in meeting the customer's sustainability goals.

Our client belatedly realized two things—it was leading with the wrong value proposition, and it had an incomplete understanding of sustainability competition. Rather than pitching that "we can help you

FIGURE 5-1

Profit protocol: Criteria for sustainability monetization

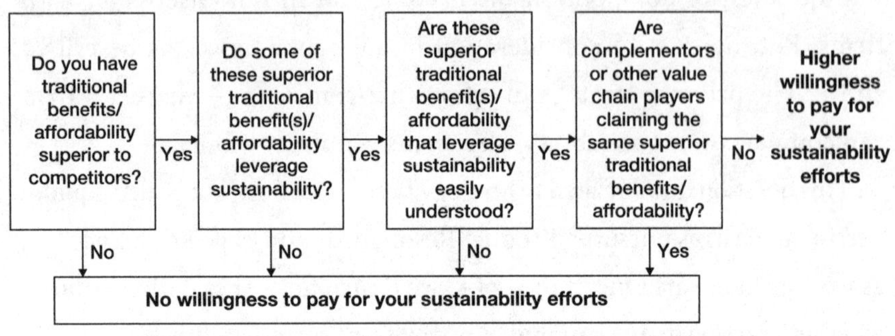
Do you have traditional benefits/ affordability superior to competitors?
Yes
Do some of these superior traditional benefit(s)/ affordability leverage sustainability?
Yes
Are these superior traditional benefit(s)/ affordability that leverage sustainability easily understood?
Yes
Are complementors or other value chain players claiming the same superior traditional benefits/ affordability?
No
Higher willingness to pay for your sustainability efforts
No
No
No
Yes
No willingness to pay for your sustainability efforts

meet your sustainability goals," they would have likely had more success by focusing on the cost savings that its energy-efficient equipment delivers. The company failed to realize that its true competitors for sustainability solutions were feed and farm-management suppliers, not equipment providers.

The example described above is not uncommon. Too many companies expect a commercial return from simply adding sustainability to their products without first testing customer willingness to pay against a rigorous framework. Our Profit Protocol provides such a framework. It allows firms to test the value of their product's sustainability benefit against four clear questions. It helps firms determine whether the addition of sustainability to their offerings is a benefit—or just another cost (figure 5-1).

Criterion 1: Do You Have Traditional Benefits/ Affordability Superior to Your Competitors?

The pursuit of sustainability can lead firms to forget simple buying dynamics. As we discussed in chapter 2, sustainability is a reason to care (RTC) and never a reason to buy (RTB). Customers buy products and services because they have a need or job to be done.

To succeed, firms must offer at least one or two highly meaningful traditional benefits—RTBs—that are superior to those of their competitors. By highly meaningful, we mean that customers prioritize them. They drive purchase. Think of quality in an automobile. Toyota is renowned because it has had the most consistent quality. About 42% of car buyers prioritize quality when making a purchase decision. Affordability is meaningful for many customers. Ryanair dominates European air travel by being the most affordable airline even though it is not always the most comfortable or convenient airline.

Think of highly meaningful traditional benefits as "non-compensatory" criteria. Great sustainability benefits or RTCs cannot overcome inferiority in these RTBs—except for, perhaps, a very tiny fraction of Super Green customers.

Criterion 2: Do Your Superior Traditional Benefit(s)/ Affordability Leverage Sustainability?

We want you to remember an adage—"the best sustainability strategies make sustainability optional." Firms are successful with sustainability when sustainability benefits are optional for customers. This is a core thesis of our book. It means that firms need to use sustainability as a catalyst to improve traditional benefits or affordability, or both. The sustainability benefits are a bonus; for example, Finish dishwasher detergent reduces water use by eliminating the need to rinse dishes.

Ideally, a firm should make sustainability investments that have the dual impact of customer value creation and sustainability. This sets the foundation for monetizing your sustainability investments.

In the case of our client mentioned above, they were the industry leaders in energy efficiency. This was a highly meaningful traditional benefit because energy costs are a large portion of the operating cost. Indeed, the operating cost dominates the capital cost associated with the equipment purchase. Winning with energy efficiency is the same as leveraging sustainability.

What if your sustainability investments do not directly impact the superior traditional benefit/affordability? It simply means that you have an "add-on" sustainability benefit—for example, eliminating plastics in packaging and replacing it with cardboard. The plain truth is that it is hard to monetize these benefits.

Criterion 3: Are Your Superior Traditional Benefit(s)/ Affordability That Leverage Sustainability Easily Understood?

Many companies lament that their sustainability efforts are invisible to customers. These efforts may be in their supply chain or manufacturing plants. They try to think of clever ways to communicate these efforts. Very few succeed because it is the wrong approach.

To belabor a point, a firm must link its sustainability investments to highly meaningful traditional benefits. But that is not enough to monetize sustainability. A firm must make the traditional benefits tangible for customers—that is, it needs to make them easily understood.

Energy savings are tangible. Finish's water savings are easily understood. But many firms fail in this respect. Food companies often use messages like "farm to fork" or "ethical and sustainable sourcing" to monetize sustainability. This is a huge mistake. These messages are not easily understood by most people. They are not connected to an RTB. Revier Cattle Company understood this. They knew their sustainability practices had a big impact on the quality of their beef. But what is quality? To make it easy for consumers to understand, Revier focused on consistency of taste. People understand what taste means.

What about sustainability investments that lead to emotional benefits? They can be made tangible as well. As every Swiss luxury watch maker knows, no one needs an expensive Swiss watch to tell the time. It is an emotional purchase. Yet, watchmakers sell luxury watches on rational criteria such as precision. The same concept applies to sustainability. Instead of luxury makers claiming the use of "eco-friendly" sourcing (which is hard to understand and monetize), they should instead focus on tangible things like scarcity, longevity, or preservation. Let's take an example of longevity and preservation.

Richemont is among the largest luxury groups with brands such as Cartier, Montblanc, and Van Cleef & Arpels. The group takes the usual actions on sustainability, such as reducing Scope 1 and 2 GHG emissions. But it also recognizes that its most positive impact is on the "S" of the ESG framework (i.e., "social"): the preservation of a heritage and nurturing of artisanal talent that would otherwise be lost forever.[26] Richemont subsidiary Vacheron Constantin's "Les Cabinotiers" collection emphasizes two attributes of performance that are easily understood, and which also have a positive sustainability impact. The first is longevity. Each watch is made to last generations. This emphasizes perpetual value over disposable luxury. The second is craftsmanship as conservation. The brand's unique watches require extreme level of hand-finishing by artisans. By imbuing their skills into their watches—rather than using cheaper mechanized methods—the company preserves centuries-old skills, supporting a cultural heritage—which is a key pillar of its sustainability narrative.

Criterion 4: Are Complementors or Other Value Chain Players Claiming the Same Superior Traditional Benefits/Affordability?

Many firms have a narrow concept of competition. The vignette about our client in the dairy equipment industry showed that the competition for monetizing sustainability was coming from the farm. This is competition from the value-chain, rather than direct competitors.

Keep in mind that for a customer GHG is GHG. It doesn't matter whether the source of lower carbon emissions is a manufacturing plant or from a farm. The key here is to be aware of the magnitude of the contribution to sustainability (i.e., the relative roles that each firm's activities play in accounting for overall emissions). A firm might be rightfully proud of its B2B offering that brings a 30% reduction in GHGs. Yet if, say, only 2% of a customer's overall GHG emissions arise from that activity, its offering will be likely eclipsed by an alternative that offers a smaller proportional reduction—say, 10%—in an activity that accounts for a large proportion (e.g., 60%) of the customer's overall emissions.

The unique aspect of sustainability is that it can create competition among complementary products. Economists define complementary goods as products whose sales are pegged to one another—tennis balls and tennis rackets; sugar and tea; cheese and crackers. Sales of one product enhance the sales of the other. Yet, in the sustainability arena, complementary products can become competitors.

Sales of detergents rise with the sales and use of washing machines. They are complementary products. Vanish, a stain remover, has the performance message of making clothes last longer. Yet this is also the message of its complementary product, the Electrolux washing machine. As part of its Better Living Program, Electrolux has modernized its technology to care better for garments, prolonging their lives.

Imagine that the customer already uses Vanish to care for her clothes. When the time comes to replace her washing machine, she might question whether it is worth paying the premium for Electrolux's low-energy, low-heat, high-care machine. She perceives that Vanish gives her many of the same benefits as the Electrolux unit, without the large capital outlay. Or the reverse may be true—if a customer has already invested in an Electrolux machine. Thus, two complementary goods risk becoming sustainability competitors.

Should Every Firm Pursue Resonance as a Strategy?

Our clients and executive education participants often ask us two common questions: Is it necessary for every firm to pursue Resonance, and which resonance strategy should they adopt?

They are often surprised when we say that not everyone should pursue Resonance. If the customer value-creation opportunities through leveraged sustainability are limited, a firm may be better off as an Operator. Perhaps, it should invest its resources elsewhere and play a pragmatic game with sustainability.

That said, we have frequently found that companies don't look hard enough at the "unwanted" outputs as a source of opportunity. They become fixated on their current path of winning. They falsely believe that there are no innovation opportunities with sustainability, when there very well might be. These are blind spots. We will dig deeper into this idea in chapter 8 to demonstrate that sustainability is often an accelerator of innovation, which is a source of competitive advantage.

A recent example of a blind spot is in the generative AI (GenAI) space. The mantra of the leading GenAI firms—such as Microsoft, Google, Amazon, Apple, Meta, Tesla, and OpenAI—was to invest in bigger models with bigger data sets and bigger data centers to process them. DeepSeek from China used open-source models to develop a model that functions almost as well as the most sophisticated models of the tech giants, but at a fraction of the cost, and a fraction of the negative sustainability externalities.[27] This is a classic example of where the tech giants had their blinders on. If they had innovated by paying attention to "unwanted" outputs, they wouldn't be scrambling today.

Another blind spot is to put pressure on suppliers to raise their sustainability standards, instead of partnering with them to build a resonance strategy. Mitr Phol, the Thailand sugar manufacturer, faced a predicament. The government of Thailand put a restriction on sugar manufacturers to procure sugarcane from within a radius of 50 kilometers of their plant. The government also fixed the selling price. While many sugar manufacturers were negotiating tough supply contracts with farmers, Mitr Phol took a different path. The company's name, which translates to "friends blossom," collaborated with farmers to improve their resource efficiency, productivity, and resilience. These efforts have resulted in 43% higher sugarcane yields, an extra $1,428 in farmer profits per hectare, and a 20% reduction in production costs per ton—while ensuring a stable and sustainable source of raw material.

Which resonance strategy to pick?

Let's consider the case of Michelin, a global leader of tires with a revenue of €27.2 billion in 2024. In 2021, Michelin's CEO, Florent Menegaux, unveiled the Michelin in Motion strategy.[28] Michelin has no intention to be an Operator.

Should Michelin focus on Product Resonance? The answer to this question lies in the size of the opportunity. Is the opportunity to deliver customer value and sustainability gains sufficiently large for the company? Tires are a category where both are possible. The rolling resistance of a tire improves fuel efficiency and cuts CO_2 emissions. More durable tires imply fewer tire replacements, leading to resource savings in the entire supply chain. EVs use heavier tires and need durability. Further, low-resistance EV tires maximize battery range.

These Product Resonance opportunities play well into Michelin's traditional strengths—the firm became a market leader through innovation. Michelin, for example, introduced the "four lives" of a tire program. Instead of replacing tires, a fleet operator customer can regroove and retread the tires to increase their longevity and reduce the total cost of ownership, with no compromise on safety. Michelin's low rolling resistance Multi-Energy Z tires, for example, achieve a 4.5% fuel economy gain.

As part of the Michelin in Motion vision, the company launched the Beyond Tires strategy that is all about Product Resonance. The idea is to invest in high-tech materials that can be sold on their own, but which also support the innovation of highest quality tires, while significantly lowering the sustainability footprint of the firm and its customers. Michelin has been investing in developing products, such as flexible composites, engineered polymers, biodegradable materials, non-toxic bioadhesives, and hydrogen fuel technology.

Should Michelin invest in Usage Resonance? As we discussed in chapter 4, the company noticed that many fleet operators were doing a poor job in maintaining tires (misuse). This was a huge customer value and sustainability opportunity because a truck's fuel consumption can increase by as much as 20% to 40% when tires are not maintained very well. This includes performing chores such as inflating tires to the right pressure, rotating tires, permuting, and repairing damaged tires. Even if Michelin had a superior tire, poor maintenance would wither away the value. Eventually, customers will wonder why they should pay a premium for the tire. The misuse by customers led Michelin to introduce Effitires, its Tire as a Service program. Going into Usage Resonance was not only a growth strategy, but crucial to Michelin's long-term survival.

Menegaux wanted to strengthen and broaden such offers. He launched the Around Tires strategy, which goes beyond selling tires.

Effitires is a part of the Around Tires strategy. But, beyond Effitires, Michelin launched services to help fleet operators optimize their operations and to provide repair services. It was customer needs that dragged Michelin into Strategic Resonance.

By 2030, Michelin in Motion aims to deliver between 20–30% of revenues from non-tire businesses (through both Around Tires and Beyond Tires), up from only 5% in 2020. This is a large and crucial Strategic Resonance opportunity. The company has made big bets in this space through a series of acquisitions of digital, telematics, and analytics firms. In Brazil, for instance, the company combines offerings such as Multi-Energy Z tires with Sascar, a telematics firm acquired by Michelin to provide fleet management services. This combined offering delivers to fleet operators a 9% fuel savings and associated CO_2 reduction. And there is Watèa as well, which we discussed earlier in the chapter as an adjacency.

We discussed three ways firms can build Resonance. These three ways—Product Resonance, Usage Resonance, and Strategic Resonance—work independently and, often, interdependently to create superior traditional benefits/affordability by using sustainability as a key lever. But how do firms enable a resonance approach? In Part 3 of the book, we focus on the role of enablers. We discuss three foundational enablers—digital, communication, and leadership—which play a crucial role in a firm developing and executing a resonance approach.

PART THREE

THE ENABLERS

6

Digital Technology and AI Enablement

Clean Winners Harness Technology

Anna, a senior executive, was introduced to the new cohort of high-potential employees at the multinational corporation's induction program by the director of learning and development, who stated, "Allow me to introduce the most important person for our sustainability strategy." One participant inquired, "So you are the chief sustainability officer?" Anna replied with a smile, "No, I'm actually the head of digital."

In chapters 3 through 5, we've explored the different types of Resonance and how firms can use them to make their sustainability strategy more successful. In this chapter and the next two, we will turn to three key enablers of such strategies: digital technology and AI, effective communications, and leadership.

We start here with digital technology and AI. You may not have realized it when you were reading the last three chapters, but digital technology and AI are common threads to all three resonance pathways; in a way, the learning and development director in our vignette was probably right when she mischievously introduced Anna, the head of digital, as the most important person for the firm's sustainability strategy.

Digital Technology and AI and Sustainability

Over the past twenty plus years, companies have integrated digital technologies into nearly everything they do. But until recently, few companies considered how digital capabilities could advance their sustainability strategies. The same could be said of AI. Most firms recognize that AI—and its foundation of data technology—is an efficiency engine. Used appropriately, AI is a transformative technology that will increase operational efficiency—this means AI will help reduce business inefficiencies and cut waste.

This does not mean digital or AI technology is a panacea. Cloud computing is more carbon intensive than the airline industry. A single data server used for cloud computing and storage consumes enough energy to power 50,000 homes.[1] To put this number in perspective, consider Ireland—21% of its total metered energy consumption went to data centers in 2023.[2] Ultimately, excess use of any resource will directly or indirectly diminish customer value or affordability.

Our colleagues from IMD, Julia Binder and Mike Wade, found that firms are using digital technologies and AI to improve their sustainability impact in three ways:[3]

- **To "see" better**—this involves using digital technology and AI to gain visibility. For example, firms are monitoring their cocoa supply by logging the journey of cocoa beans from growers' cooperatives to supermarket shelves.

- **To act better**—this involves using digital technology and AI along with associated data technologies, to make better decisions. BASF's Digital Farming harnesses a suite of sensors, satellites, drones, and GPS mapping that allows farmers to use AI tools to analyze soil quality and crop health in real-time and to help them make better decisions to optimize yield.

- **To scale better**—by 2030, all plastic packaging sold in the EU must be recyclable. The Holy Grail 2.0 initiative digitizes the sorting process for post-consumer packaging waste. It will establish an open and interoperable system for retailers, packaging suppliers, waste management firms, and recyclers. The system should enhance the sorting of plastic waste into the correct material stream.

Digital Technology and AI as Resonance Enablers

Too often Operators, Strivers, and Enthusiasts use digital and AI technologies to address sustainability problems at scale. Resonators, in contrast, use digital and AI technologies to solve customer value problems at scale, but with a sustainability lens. Clean Winners leverage digital and AI technologies for achieving the three types of Resonance.

Digital Technology and AI as Enablers of Product Resonance

Digital technology can provide precise solutions for customers using data and AI. Companies—such as the insurer Discovery, ecommerce retailer Pinduoduo, and John Deere—leverage these technologies to supercharge customer value and sustainability. Let's see them in action.

Personalizing health insights

Discovery faced spiraling costs in its native South Africa. Its business was hampered by a high disease burden and an inability to select members, due to government antidiscrimination regulations.

Its visionary founder, Adrian Gore, saw that many health insurance firms were engaged in sustainability projects with corporate social responsibility in mind, such as education programs or free clinics for the poor. These initiatives were often disconnected from the business. He embraced the idea of creating customer value and societal value simultaneously by interlinking them. He shifted Discovery's focus to *prevention* of disease.

The shift to prevention meant that the company had to encourage its members toward healthier lifestyles—curbing alcohol intake and smoking, while embracing a healthier diet and exercise. This is easier said than done. Most members recognized the lifestyle changes necessary to improve their health. Yet the popularity of slogans like "you only live once," the perception of healthy foods as costly, and a general view of exercise as time-consuming or expensive, presented barriers to people making the change.

In the face of these barriers, Discovery knew education alone was insufficient. Thus, in 1997, it created a health insurance program called Vitality. Vitality is built on a foundation of using digital technologies and AI to enable massive member (customer) participation.

The Vitality program incentivized behavioral changes by giving members rewards for making small lifestyle changes and achieving health goals. For example, if a Vitality customer attends regular health checkups with their doctor, they receive discounts on health food purchases or gym memberships. Discovery integrated this activity loop into a product feature called Vitality Points, under which members receive points for healthy lifestyle choices. After they pass a certain points threshold, members unlock better rewards.

Discovery's gambits became bolder. Digitalization and AI were its winning play. Discovery's AI algorithms frequently use insights from behavioral economics to nudge members toward desired behaviors. For example, the firm used the insight of "loss aversion" (i.e., people prefer to avoid losing something over winning) to encourage more frequent exercise. The firm gave an Apple Watch to customers for a small upfront fee. To avoid paying further down payments for the timepiece (i.e., a "loss"), participants had to engage in healthy activities and earn Vitality points. After accumulating enough points, they could keep their watch.

The behavior-change initiative was effective. A study of 400,000 Vitality customers across three countries revealed that Vitality's smartwatch strategy had caused its most engaged customers to increase their physical activity by 34%.

The company also formed partnerships with select grocery stores. Members could use an app to scan a product to know whether it was healthy. If a product was unhealthy, the app would recommend an alternative. Members also got automatic discounts at checkout if they purchased healthy foods. This was only possible because Discovery integrated its IT systems with those of the grocery stores.

The Vitality program's overall impact on customer health has been remarkable. Discovery's 2024 annual report shows that the gambit toward prevention is working. The company has greater persistency (42% lower lapses) and a 9% reduction in claims. The impact of the behavioral changes increases with age. While a moderately healthy 30-year-old gets a 7% increase in lifespan, for a 70-year-old it is 90% (from 6.1 years to 11.6 years).

. . .

Besides delivering better product value, businesses use digital technology and AI to create interconnected platforms. These platforms provide shared networks for users, merchants, and other actors who can freely exchange value with each other, which would have otherwise been impossible. Pinduoduo is a shining example of this.

Helping farmers become entrepreneurs

Pinduoduo is one of the largest ecommerce platforms in China. The company launched in 2015. By 2023, it had more than 600 million active monthly users.[4] And its revenues reached $34 billion.[5] Pinduoduo achieved such rapid success at scale by inventing a unique playing field—group or team buying.[6] The Pinduoduo model is based on the inclusion of those who were excluded by traditional ecommerce players such as Alibaba.

On the digital platform, users can buy individually at regular prices—or buy the same product as a group for a discount. The pricing mechanism incentivizes consumers to share and encourage their friends to buy together, which helps promote merchants' products and create greater sales volumes. The gamification of buying, digital payments, and a cartless recommendation system all power the fun team-shopping experience. Moreover, merchants' products are priced affordably. The offering attracted underserved customers in China's smaller cities, which were high growth areas.[7]

The true power of Pinduoduo comes from bringing farmers and merchants (sellers) and customers closer than before by reconfiguring the supply chain. Its merchant-to-customer model helped farmers turn into entrepreneurs, having a vast social impact. By eliminating middlemen and enabling farmers to sell their produce to customers, farmers increased their profit margins, while customers got better product options (better customer value). Pinduoduo's AI models even help farmers with optimal pricing of their goods.

Pinduoduo doubled down on farming impact through its Duo Duo Farm program. Under the initiative, the company worked with local administrations and expert partners to train and support farmers. The training helped farmers optimize their produce harvest with new techniques and equipment. It also helped them improve their packaging to reduce waste. Pinduoduo says it connected with 16 million farmers, and a total of 61 billion orders were placed on its platform in 2021.[8] In 2022, the company won the UN Food and Agriculture Organization Award for Innovation for its digital solution to lifting the livelihoods of farmer by connecting them directly to consumers.[9]

Meeting the needs of farmers

John Deere illustrates how firms can use enhancements to current products—in this case, agricultural equipment—to add value to customers. It had revenues of $61 billion and net income of nearly $10 billion in 2023.[10] It is one of the world's largest agricultural equipment manufacturers.

The company embraced digital in the 1990s. Its vision was to make farming more efficient. Over the years, as sustainability became a key concern for farming, precision agriculture has become an imperative. Making this shift would have been impossible if the company had not laid the foundations for digital technology and AI back when it did.

The most exciting innovation by John Deere is to devolve precision agriculture to the plant level. Think about a farmer growing corn. A single acre is typically home to 13,000–37,000 plants. The idea that John Deere can manage each plant individually seems outlandish.

Yet the company's See & Spray technology, which is a feature of its tractor, enables exactly that. It uses computer vision and AI to identify weeds—and apply herbicide directly on individual plants. This is a far cry from spraying chemicals on entire farms to kill weeds. The technology saved nearly 80 million gallons of chemical application on farms in 2023.[11] This amounted to a 59% reduction in herbicide use by its US farmer customers.[12] The farmers save money by using less herbicide. They save time through precision spraying. They also reduce soil and water contamination from chemicals.

John Deere is essentially competing with complementary products in the value chain such as herbicides, even though it does not make these products.

Smart Apply, another digital enabler, uses intelligent spray systems that employ light detection and ranging (LIDAR). This scans tree-foliage densities in real time and automatically decides where to spray chemical solutions.[13] This system can reduce chemical runoff by 93%

and water use by 50%. It reduces input costs for farmers—and keeps farmlands healthy by reducing contamination.[14]

Digital Technology and AI as Enablers of Usage Resonance

Leveraging digital technology and AI allows firms to create new usage models that would be infeasible without these innovations. This is about expanding the company's products and services to help solve problems related to misuse, underuse, or overuse, in ways that add customer value and enhance sustainability.

Making buildings better for customers

Johnson Controls is a building energy and efficiency solutions company founded in 1885. It is a huge player—its products and services are found in more than 1 million buildings and its sales totaled $26.79 billion in 2023.[15] It operates in the building industry, which is a major contributor to carbon pollution, as nearly 40% of all global carbon emissions come from the building sector.

Given their impact on sustainability, building owners and operators are under pressure to reduce carbon emissions in their operations. Moreover, the COVID-19 pandemic triggered public health concerns over hygiene in workspaces.

Johnson Controls saw an opportunity to use data to improve both the efficiency and healthiness of its buildings. It launched its OpenBlue platform—which runs on a Software as a Service (SaaS) model.[16]

OpenBlue is an interconnected system that monitors all key building data in real-time. This includes data from HVAC systems, fire control and safety instruments, sensors, equipment, energy utilities, and weather forecasts.[17] It then uses machine-learning algorithms to analyze and generate real-time insights on user experience and sustainability.[18] The system helps optimize parameters like energy efficiency and indoor air quality. Meanwhile, customers gain enhanced security, predictive maintenance, and reduced operating costs.

The OpenBlue digitization was the conduit for Johnson to an adjacency. Its original playing field was equipment provision. Yet, through digitization, it entered an adjacent arena—that of digital-service provision for customer buildings. "In 2023, OpenBlue Enterprise Manager and OpenBlue Central Utility Plant helped our customers avoid an estimated 70,000 metric tons of CO_2, more than four times the avoided emissions of 2020," Johnson Controls said in 2024.[19]

Creating new usage models via digital

Recall our Resonator Michelin from chapter 4. The French motoring giant morphed from selling tires to providing tire maintenance services to tackling future mobility challenges.[20]

Now, Michelin has embraced digital to augment its resonator strategy even further. Its Connected Fleet service serves more than 50,000 customers. The tire company is now also a global fleet strategist.

Michelin Connected Fleet service, which is a subscription-based model, uses digital telematics to collect real-time vehicle performance data and AI to optimize performance. In the form of key performance indicators (KPIs), the data is used to share analytics and insights with customers. Businesses gain improved tire and fleet optimization, as well as enhanced fleet operation performance.

Consider the real-world benefits. Connected Fleet's software optimization allows customer fleet vehicles to use the most efficient logistics routes for timely and fuel-efficient deliveries. This reduces customers' fleet fuel costs *and* lowers emissions.

Connected Fleet's smart braking system alerts drivers if vehicle brakes are not performing well. This saves fuel costs over time and enhances driver safety. The system also features smart predictive tire maintenance—which further reduces the risk of accidents.

Digital Technology and AI as Enablers of Strategic Resonance

Digital technology and AI can facilitate a firm's move into adjacent playing fields, which they might otherwise have hesitated to go into.

Creating opportunities for network effects

In the early 2000s, less than 10% of the Kenyan population had access to banking. Yet 50% had cell phone connectivity. Safaricom, a major mobile network provider in Kenya spotted an opportunity.

In 2007, it built a digital payment platform with its majority owner, Vodafone. The platform was called M-PESA.[21] Its goal was to improve financial inclusion and provide easy access to financial services for its users, especially the underprivileged—the unbanked. M-PESA made it possible to connect a user's account with their SIM card. This enabled cashless digital transactions without needing a bank account.

The M-Pesa system has been enhanced since its inception. It now offers international transactions. It provides tools such as application programming interfaces (APIs) to partners and business owners worldwide. These allow businesses to integrate M-PESA as a payment option, which enables customer-to-business and business-to-business transactions.[22]

M-PESA has created social value of $2 billion in Kenya alone. It has delivered 250,000 jobs in the country and given 20 million rural inhabitants financial access.[23] Furthermore, it now powers more than 300 digital services for the Kenyan government, helping the government save millions of dollars.[24]

Kenya was just the beginning. Today, M-Pesa serves eight African countries. It handles more than $1 billion of transaction volume for its 60 million users.[25] It now brands itself a "super app." It has the ambition to justify that billing—it aims to expand its financial services into sectors like insurance, and into territories such as South America.

In 2012, M-PESA partnered with NCBA Bank Kenya to deliver a savings and lending service called M-Shwari.[26] Via a simple savings account, users could take small monthly loans to fulfill their financial needs and build a credit history.[27] M-PESA accomplished this by using an extensive set of data parameters from sources like M-PESA usage, lending history, and so forth to devise a credit score for its users. More diversification and expansion beckon. "When you look at how much money is sitting on the M-PESA ecosystem that has not been intermediated on, you see a huge opportunity for us to disintermediate on that with partners," says M-PESA chairman Sitoyo Lopokoiyit. "We're looking at more of a platform play, whether it's insurance or wealth management."[28]

. . .

In chapter 5, we explored Mahindra Group's new business vertical, Krish-e. Mahindra launched Krish-e to help farmers (especially smallholders) prosper by improving their farming practices. "There are two things that it does fundamentally: it offers value-added services around advisory and around rental," says Ramesh Ramachandran, senior VP and head of Krish-e at Mahindra. "It has a physical as well as a digital face and all this is powered by innovations around technology."[29]

Krish-e harnesses digital technology and AI to deliver customized, plot-specific guidance on better cropping and harvesting procedures, weather, and pest updates to farmers via an app. The app also features a digital marketplace that gives farmers access to agricultural resources.

Mahindra has also launched a hardware offering called Krish-e Smart Kit. This gives farmers digital farm-monitoring capabilities. The kit connects farming equipment with GPS, capturing accurate farm activity, then relaying it to farmers' smartphones. It can be used with any farm equipment brand. It also features a digital marketplace where farmers can rent machinery through a pay-per-use model. Many farmers are unable to afford expensive high-performance equipment. Yet the rental platform helps them access such machinery.[30]

Amplifying Resonance Through Digital Technology and AI

Our research and interviews revealed several core principles that Resonators use to support their sustainability and customer value efforts through digital technology and AI. We explore them here.

Principle 1: Gather Insights into the full customer journey

Michelin, Schneider Electric, Mahindra Group, Discovery, and John Deere don't just focus on the products they sell. They look beyond their products to gather further insights into customer problems in their end-to-end journey.

This broader lens allows them to discover a key customer insight—which is that many of their customers had troublesome end-to-end journeys. Current customer practices, as well as products and services by third parties, were often rife with inefficiencies and waste. This meant there was an opportunity to leverage sustainability to create customer value.

Michelin exemplifies this thinking. The company was established to make and sell tires. It was largely uninvolved in how customers *used* their tires. When the firm explored customers' problems in using tires, it discovered that customer maintenance personnel often did a poor job monitoring tire air pressure, rotating tires, or retreading and regrooving them on time. These poor customer practices led to increased fuel consumption and higher tire repair frequency, which meant higher carbon emissions as well.

With these pain points identified, Michelin expanded its presence in its customers' journeys. Michelin Connected Fleet addressed these specific customer value and sustainability problems.

The lesson here is simple. Don't look at your products through a narrow lens. Most firms say they do customer journeys, but what they really do is the journey of their product. Your product journey is not a customer journey.

Principle 2: Implement customer value measurement tools, not just sustainability measurement tools

Myriad companies have built measurement tools, such as carbon emission calculators, to demonstrate sustainability gains. Yet they often miss the crucial need to build similar tools to demonstrate customer value on traditional benefits and affordability.

Resonators like Discovery and Johnson Controls have done both.

Discovery's Vitality program is made available to customers through a mobile app. Every member's journey is digitally tracked—from their exercise patterns to food purchases.

At Johnson Controls, CTO Vijay Sankaran says, "Everything that we're doing here is intrinsically aligned to driving energy efficiency. So, one of the things that we have in the tools is ROI calculators for energy conservation. You can go in and ask, if I took this action, what would be the ROI?"[31]

Charlotte Degot, CEO of CO2 AI, which is helping firms measure their carbon emissions using Generative AI (GenAI), noted a difference between Resonators and others. In her view, too many large firms are making decisions to reduce carbon emissions with highly inaccurate measurements. And these decisions are often made with little consideration for the impact on customer value. This is a double whammy.

Reckitt is using GenAI to obtain precise emissions data for each of its 25,000 products. The firm has achieved a 75-fold improvement in the accuracy of its emissions footprint measurement. Reckitt's purchasing function is equipped with this data, which helps them make the right trade-offs between sustainability and customer value.

Principle 3: Build slowly but systematically

Providing the dual benefit of traditional *and* sustainability value is an ambitious endeavor. Digital technology and AI can make it happen—but it is a slow process with plenty of bumps along the way. Be ready to adapt and evolve your approach. Be ready to build new capabilities through partnerships and acquisitions.

John Deere's story of using digital technology and AI is one of constant evolution. The company has always focused on making farming productive and profitable for its customers. As new digital technologies emerged over the past 25 years, Deere continually improved its capabilities to deliver more efficient farming solutions. How did it make this happen?

During the 1990s, Deere established an internal group of engineers and data scientists to explore opportunities for growth through digital technologies. The group was called the Intelligent Solutions Group. Through the developments made under the initiative, Deere acquired NavCom Technology in 1999. This allowed it to deliver a new GPS-based farm-management system to its customers in the early 2000s. The system functioned by fitting tractors with GPS. This helped farmers perform farm operations more efficiently by avoiding redundant field passes. The technology improved the fuel efficiency of the equipment by up to 40%.[32]

These promising results encouraged Deere to carve its efforts and acquisitions into a multi-year strategy. In 2013, Deere launched the "Farm Forward Vision," which aimed to use digital technology to give farmers better insights. These insights would help them manage their farms more effectively—even remotely. They could operate farm equipment while sitting in their cabin through Deere's digital solutions. This enhanced productivity.

Deere recognized the rapid developments in integrated techniques, such as machine-learning, AI, and computer vision. In 2017, it acquired AI and robotics startup Blue River Technologies for $305 million. Blue River developed See & Spray robots that could precisely apply fertilizers to specific plants on the farm.[33]

The acquisition helped Deere launch its AI-focused Farm Forward Vision 2.0. "It's very clear that we need to be on the vanguard of these technologies," a senior VP at the John Deere Intelligent Solutions Group said. "There's a lot of economic upside and profitability as well as sustainability that can be unlocked for farmers through them."[34]

Today, the company boasts more than 650,000 digitally connected machines. Almost 400 million acres of farmland are served by Deere's digital solutions. With such a strong presence in precision agriculture, John Deere holds a formidable position with a market worth $150 billion.[35]

Principle 4: Share digital layers

Digital technology has the potential to deliver customer value and sustainability gains at scale. Rather than leveraging digital technology and AI sporadically, firms can put these technologies at the core of their business, enabling connections between and among product offerings in order to enhance value. Clean Winners like John Deere (through its Operations Center), Schneider Electric (through its EcoStruxure platform) and Honeywell (through its Connected Enterprise) are already doing this for their customers.

In the previous section, we explored precision-agriculture technologies such as See & Spray. Here, digital technology is used in the product itself (e.g., a tractor). But its application extends further. John Deere's diverse range of agricultural equipment share a common trait—they generate data when used. John Deere captures this data through its Operations Center, which is an online farm management system. This is its "shared digital layer," which puts all the data inputs generated by farm-level equipment into the hands of farmers on simple dashboards. Farmers can then make efficient choices for farm management.

If a farmer uses Deere's technology, data from the field is recorded in the Operations Center. The term "engaged acres" is used by Deere to refer to the acreage utilizing this technology. Deere's equipment collects data from 388 million engaged acres. This data helps farmers optimize their productivity. This data has helped farmers reduce overall carbon emissions by 9% and improve crop efficiency by 7%.

Honeywell is another firm that has developed a shared digital layer across its businesses and applied it to sustainability. The US firm, founded in 1905, has helped customers with automation in aviation, energy, building, and other areas. In 2023, Honeywell had net sales of nearly $36 billion. Its operating income was $7 billion.[36]

Darius Adamczyk became chief executive of Honeywell in 2017. He wanted to evolve Honeywell from a traditional industrial firm to one that uses software and AI extensively. Honeywell had four core business areas—aviation, building, energy, and industrial automation. The company built a common digital platform shared by the four businesses called Honeywell Connected Enterprise (HCE). The common platform, installed on customer sites, made it easier to collect data on its equipment. Said data provided insights to improve efficiency, reduce carbon emissions, and minimize downtimes through predictive maintenance.[37]

Software-based solutions from HCE have recorded 25% annual recurring sales growth since 2019. More than 50% of HCE revenues arise from its SaaS business model.[38] This enables the firm to deliver customer value and sustainability simultaneously, not just at a product level, but across an entire portfolio of products.

Principle 5: Be mindful of the double-edge sword

Digital technologies can make the customer experience easier. They can also make it more uncomfortable. Firms must be mindful of this dichotomy—particularly as interconnected digital products and services become commonplace for their organization.

Take M-PESA, for example. It fostered financial inclusion for underprivileged groups in Africa through the simplicity of its digital payment platform. Customers simply need a phone with a SIM card to make digital transactions. This makes it easier for underprivileged users, who might otherwise lack access to the digital economy. For M-PESA, this simple onboarding helps extend its reach to ever-greater numbers of people. It already has over 60 million users.

By standardizing its platform, M-PESA is removing the ceiling to success at scale. "We need to have a standardized platform that is 90% common across all our markets," said M-PESA chairman Sitoyo Lopokoiyit. "That is the role M-PESA Africa is playing. The mission is to build standardized digital platforms—so we are working hard to ensure that we have a common platform."[39]

Yet digitalization can go wrong. Indeed, it prompted a class action lawsuit at John Deere. We have learned of the benefits that Deere's precision agriculture equipment can bring to the farm level. But this functionality demanded tighter digital integration with farming equipment, which made repairs less accessible for customers.

Deere's precision agriculture equipment uses an engine control unit (ECU), which imposes a software lock on the repair and maintenance of the equipment. Thus, customers were unable to perform self-repairs or use third-party service firms. Customers lacked access to repair modules, documentation, or the technical inputs needed to repair equipment. Only Deere itself could access these key internals. It was sued in 2022 for creating an illegal monopoly.[40]

But it did recover. In 2023, Deere settled the dispute by signing a memorandum of understanding with the contesting parties. Under the agreement, Deere now shares the required documentations and technical know-how with farmers, restoring their access to equipment repair.[41]

Digitization is a powerful enabler, but firms must always be considering impacts to the customer experience, and be sensitive to the potential hazards.

The Digital Dividend

In this chapter, we saw how digital technology and AI can powerfully enhance customer value and sustainability simultaneously, enabling firms to become Resonators. The five principles—improve customer journeys; implement digital measuring; build slowly but systematically; share digital layers; remember the double-edge sword—provide a useful guide for leveraging digital technology and AI to forge a path to a future that is both profitable and sustainable.

In chapter 7, we explore another enabler—and show how Clean Winners communicate.

7

Communications Enablement

Clean Winners Message Smartly

Michael was puzzled. An engineer at a German food equipment supplier, he had been working for several months on a new spray dryer for small to medium-sized food companies. He was reading the Indian subsidiary's marketing leaflet about his product. While the document duly highlighted the 20–30% operating cost savings, it omitted that the unit could also reduce carbon emissions by 50%. He wondered why such a key benefit was left out. How could they miss this selling point?

American firms spend half a trillion dollars annually on marketing for a reason: Unless customers are aware of an offering's benefits, they are unlikely to buy it.[1] Building that awareness through communication is the key to success—both at the product and the corporate levels.

Traditional sustainability strategies each use a rather straightforward playbook to create opportunities that correspond to the role they assign to sustainability. And with opportunities comes the varying risk of greenwashing. By contrast, Clean Winners' use of communication is more subtle. At the product level, they find a specific path through the five "uncomfortable truths" (chapter 2) and make communication contingent on the specific market situation. Michael will find his answer there. At the corporate level, they leverage communication as a tool to further integrate sustainability in their corporate strategy.

Product-Level Sustainability Communication

A communication strategy typically involves three dimensions: goal, intensity, and execution strategy[2]. For sustainability communication, however, a fourth dimension must be considered: the extent to which the firm is engaging in green- and social-washing.[3]

The first dimension is the communication goal: What objective does the firm pursue when communicating about sustainability? Generally, there are two types of messages.[4] "Upper-funnel" messages aim to create awareness, desire, and/or interest for the product or the firm, with the goal of progressively building the brand and influencing customers' perceptions for future sales. In contrast, "lower-funnel" messages aim to achieve the short-term goal of driving sales. The objective here is to influence purchases or encourage a specific behavior, such as clicking a "call to action" on a digital ad button, to provide contact information.

The second dimension involves determining the communication intensity of the sustainability strategy. Firms must decide the degree to which the sustainability theme will be emphasized in the communication. This may vary from being the central focus of the communication piece, to being highlighted through a certification logo and brief descriptions, or being mentioned as a small footnote in fine print, if at all.

The third traditional dimension is the communication execution, which involves deciding how to communicate with customers. This can be divided into two "routes" or ways to persuade customers.[5] The "direct route" engages customers in a logical, cognitive process about the merits of the argument. For example, in sustainability, this might involve using explanations, diagrams, and numbers to demonstrate that the product's manufacture process reduces CO_2 emissions or has a positive impact on communities. Research shows that this method is the most effective method of persuasion. However, it would be impossible to carefully think through every piece of communication one sees; the central route only works if customers are (1) willing and (2) able to process the message. Alternatively, the "peripheral route" should be used. That route relies on cues or associations that influence customers without requiring them to engage deeply. For instance, showing windmills in a pristine environment or featuring a sustainability label can serve as peripheral cues.

In addition to these three classical dimensions, sustainability communication must come to grips with the issue of greenwashing. The malaise is widespread. In North America, a Google survey among chief experience officers (CXOs) showed that 72% of respondents felt that their organization has overstated its sustainability effort.[6] In 2020, an EU Commission special report revealed that 53% of environmental claims were potentially misleading, and 42% of them may be false or deceptive.[7]

Greenwashing is a sleight of hand: the act of communicating positively about environmental or social performance, while failing to act accordingly. Greenwashing is the mother of a family of ploys that share a common characteristic: a desire to hoodwink the consumer (or investors) into believing a product, service, or company has a better sustainability profile than it actually does in reality.[8]

Myriad factors conspire to prompt the use of greenwashing.[9] The trading landscape in which a firm operates is key. Industries and countries characterized by lax, unprecise, and uncertain rules and regulations are, for example, fertile ground for the practice, particularly where consumers and investors place pressure on firms to appear sustainable.[10] Organizational-level drivers, such as the ethical climate and the incentive structure for key leaders, also play a role. Mentality is another key factor; leaders with a short-term mindset and/or an optimism bias are more likely to approve greenwashed campaigns.

While we have not met many leaders who openly defended the idea of greenwashing, it remains a thorny topic, as managers frequently exhibit double standards. They accuse their competitors of greenwashing and then berate their own marketing and communication teams for failing to shout about their own sustainability agenda.

Let's see how firms play with these four dimensions to promote their sustainable actions.

Traditional product sustainability strategies

Recall that *Operators* are firms who invest conservatively in a few sustainability initiatives in order to keep their license to operate. When Operators communicate these initiatives, their objective is pretty simple: It is a message of reassurance, convincing customers that they are *compliant* on sustainability. Aside from that simple messaging, they focus on Reasons to Buy (RTBs). Depending on the situation, their sustainability communication intensity is low to medium—they talk about sustainability rather infrequently. In terms of execution, Operators don't waste much time or space with visual "green" cues suggesting that they are sustainability active, and they don't engage customers with precise arguments either. Their sustainability claims are vague enough so that critics will be unable to challenge them.

The Chinese fast-fashion brand Shein is an Operator. The sustainability messaging on its product pages is heavily subordinate to RTBs like price, fit, and look. When such messaging is found, it is indefinable—for example making meaningless claims like "T-shirt made with 30% preferred materials," without specifying what "preferred" really means.[11] This vagueness is a typical instance of greenwashing (i.e., "deceptive manipulation"—the intentional use of unverified claims and statements), and Operators do their share of greenwashing. However, because they do speak a little about Reasons to Care (RTCs), they are probably not the main offenders overall.

Strivers limit their sustainability investment, but they view sustainability as a megatrend that cannot be ignored. They think RTCs are a great way of attracting the attention of customers, thus their message relies heavily on them. Their fondness for RTCs can cause them to take undue risks: they communicate RTCs aggressively. They shout about RTCs even to the point of guilt-tripping—favoring "buy now because you care" lower-funnel messaging. Their communication intensity is similarly bold. They frequently stretch their sustainability claims to attract customers, communicating RTCs in tandem with RTBs. Their communication execution is audacious—using highly visible, superficial campaigns that use peripheral cues like thriving plants and happy animals to show how sustainable they are. In 2022, the US beverage brewing system company Keurig was fined both in the United States and in Canada for advertising that its pods were "recyclable" (the claim "Have your cup and recycle it, too" figured in large type), when the pods where actually not accepted for recycling in many areas.[12]

Enthusiasts put sustainability at the heart of everything they do, and they are convinced that RTCs are a great way to attract customers. But, unlike Strivers, they have learned to be more careful by codifying their message and following guidelines to eliminate possible accusations of greenwashing. Enthusiasts want to be market leaders on sustainability. Their communication goal typically focuses on upper-funnel messaging, as they are looking for long-term perception gains and reputation benefits.

Their messaging on RTCs is so intense it can sometimes crowd out the RTBs: The sustainability message is put front and center, overwhelming the communication on the job to be done. The higher-purpose messaging would very often read something like: "We are in this together to save the planet and make the world a better place. Buy our products to show you are leading the pack." They integrate RTCs into the raison d'être of their product and expect consumers to make rational, cognitive assessments of their message, rather than respond to superficial, peripheral cues. Consider Unilever. Campaigns like Dove refillable deodorant focused on RTCs (waste reduction) rather than RTBs (smelling good). By our own count, RTBs such as 48-hour odor protection, fresh smell, or being hypoallergenic occupy only about 25% of the video ad's time.[13]

Clean Winners product communication

Clean Winners' points of departure are the five "uncomfortable truths" (chapter 2): Sustainability does not trigger purchases, most customers do not care about sustainability, some sustainability features are a liability, sustainability trade-offs are unusual and difficult for customers to make, and sustainability does not often directly result in higher prices. They know that promoting products on their sustainability benefits—RTCs—is a contingent strategy. It can work. But only under certain conditions.

We propose a three-stage process (see figure 7-1). The first stage consists of analyzing the market "color" composition in each product market and its evolution: How many are Super Greens, Greens, Blues, Grays, and Ultra Grays? The proportion will change over time, so the assessments must be dynamic and ongoing. Clean Winners recognize that they cannot change the world. It is not their role to *increase the proportion* of Greens in the customer mix, but merely to quantify it so their communication can be effective.

Ideally, firms would tailor their sustainability messaging based on the proportion of Greens and Super Greens. In markets with few Greens, they would use only RTB-focused communication—called *Standard Communication* (Strategy 1 on the flowchart)—since promoting RTCs is ineffective for disinterested audiences.

If there are enough Green consumers, one possibility is for the firm to focus its communication efforts on RTCs. However, as discussed in

FIGURE 7-1

Clean Winners communications strategy

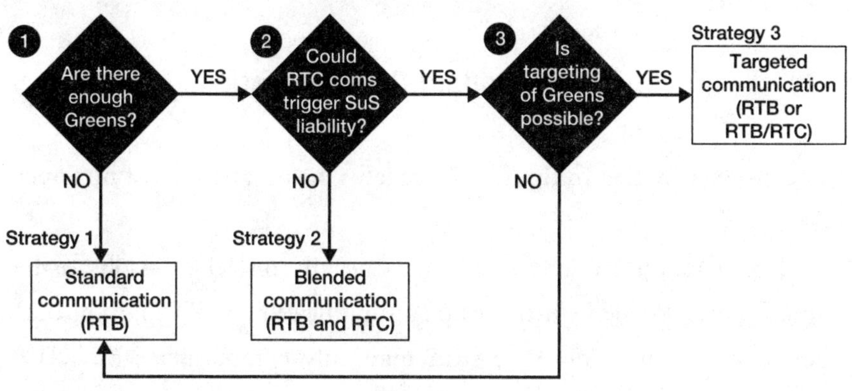

Note: RTB: Reasons to buy; RTC: Reasons to care; SuS: sustainability.

chapter 2, sustainability initiatives may also decrease perceived value among non-Green consumers. In such cases, promoting RTCs could potentially lead to reduced engagement from Blues and Grays, which may offset gains among Greens.

The second stage of the process entails determining whether RTC communication may give rise to sustainability liability. If no such risk is present, organizations may proceed to implement Strategy 2: *Blended Communication*. In this approach, RTBs and RTCs are integrated and conveyed concurrently.

So what do you do if you have enough Greens, but a suspicion that communicating about sustainability could decrease the value of the product for the non-Greens? Step three consists of examining whether you can develop communication assets that specifically target the Greens. If this is the case, firms adopt Strategy 3 on the flowchart: *Targeted Communication*. If, however, they feel unable to master such targeting, they act pragmatically—and instead resort to Standard Communication.

Let's dig deeper and illustrate the three communication strategies. The central key question is: How much of their communication should focus on sustainability (RTCs) versus traditional messaging (RTBs) for each segment?

Type 1: Standard Communication

The product-market in figure 7-2 has few Greens, and almost no Super Greens.

Here, communications must focus heavily on RTBs—"jobs to be done." There should be little or no communication on RTCs. In its outbound communications, the firm may only communicate on RTCs face-to-face with the handful of Green customers it has. Meanwhile, in its inbound communications, sustainability will likely be buried somewhere on the website. An example of such a market is a German B2B

FIGURE 7-2

Standard communication strategy

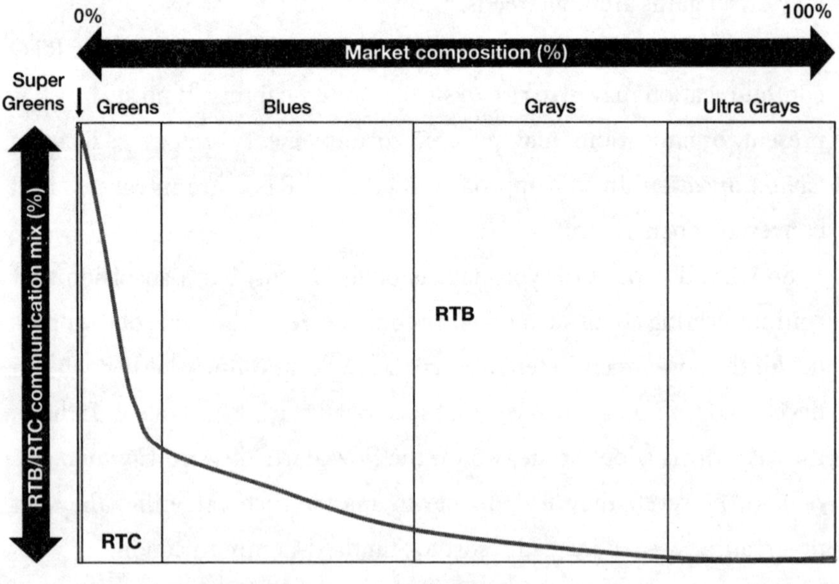

Note: RTB: Reasons to buy; RTC: Reasons to care.

system supplier for the food and beverage industry in India. Remember the introduction to this chapter? This is where Michael is employed. Sustainability is a lesser concern for the Indian public than in richer Western nations.[14] For this firm, India is an example where communications on RTCs should be minimal.

It is important to note that Standard Communication also serves as a pragmatic approach in situations when Greens are present, but where it is not easy to target them separately, and when RTC communication may pose sustainability liabilities.

Type 2: Blended Communication

The product-market in Figure 7-3 is evenly distributed across customer types.

FIGURE 7-3

Blended communication strategy

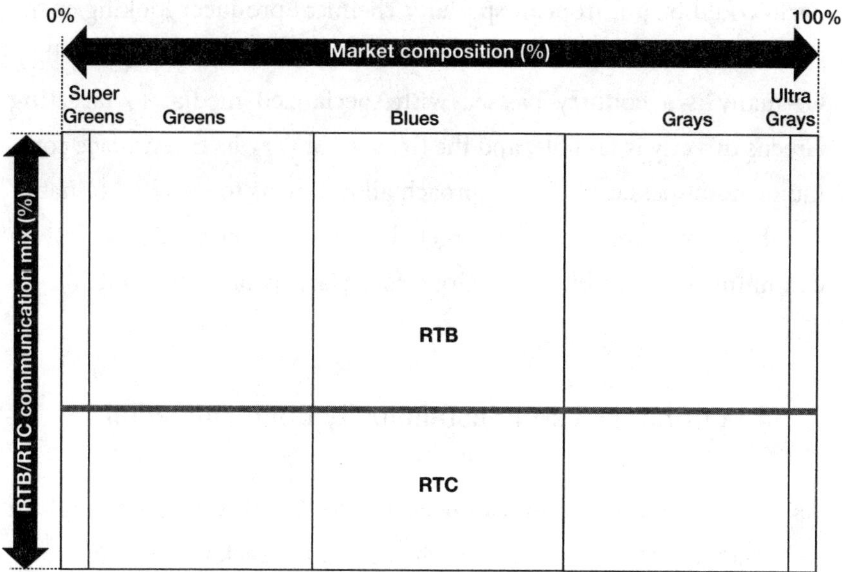

RTB: Reasons to buy; RTC: Reasons to care

Blended Communication involves intertwining RTBs and RTCs and communicating on them across the entire market simultaneously. In this scenario, firms should communicate simultaneously on RTBs *and* RTCs across the board. There is no need to tweak the communication mix to promote RTCs to Greens and RTBs to Blues and Grays: every message should go to all at once. Yet a blended strategy only works in markets where sustainability liability is unlikely. A classic example of this is the US market for organic cotton bedding. Sustainability liability is unlikely here because a key functional attribute of cotton is its softness and kindness to skin.

Type 3: Targeted Communication

The third type of market also has plenty of targetable Greens (figure 7-4). In this case, communications must be carefully directed. Both RTC *and* RTB messaging is pushed to Greens. The rest of the market receives primarily RTB-only communications. An example of this scenario could be a European specialty chemical producer looking at the German market. Some, but not all, clients will care about sustainability. Germany is a country blessed with specialized media, so targeting Greens directly is feasible, and the firm could vary its face-to-face communication messages. This approach allows firms to avoid sustainability liability—Greens are targeted directly with RTCs, while communications to Blues and Grays focus largely or solely on RTBs.

Corporate-Level Sustainability Communication

As we have seen, communicating sustainability to consumers can be a risky pursuit. The same is true at the corporate level, where firms communicate with all their stakeholders, including employees, NGOs, communities, investors, regulators, suppliers, etc. Whereas traditional

FIGURE 7-4

Targeted communication strategy

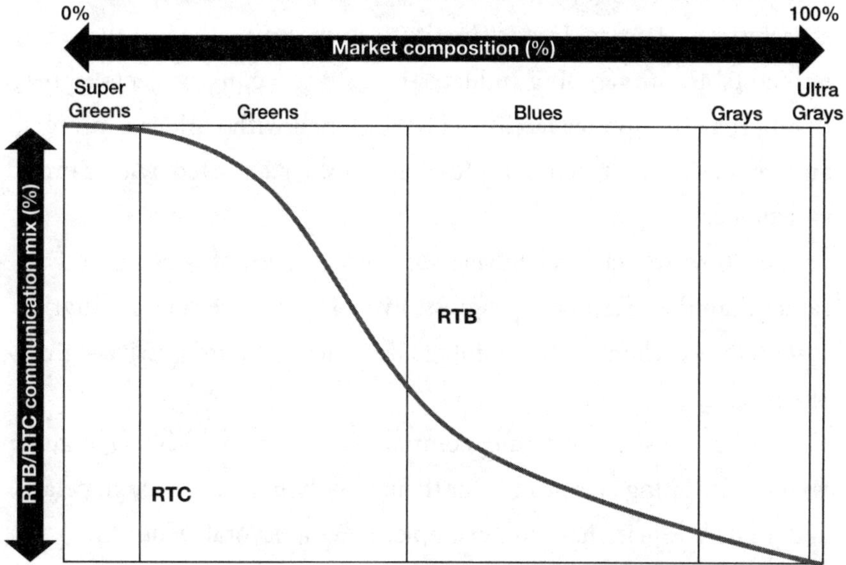

Note: RTB: Reasons to buy; RTC: Reasons to care.

strategies consist of *highlighting some elements* of a firm's sustainability activities, Clean Winners take a different approach so as to *integrate* sustainability into their strategy—and make it contingent on the industry and/or message complexity.

Traditional corporate sustainability strategies

To put it simply, Operators will highlight their (few) initiatives, Strivers will highlight the progress they have been making, and Enthusiasts will highlight the purpose that drives their overall strategy.

Operators have their own model for showcasing the organization of their sustainability activities. However, they will typically focus their corporate communication on a handful of sustainability initiatives. Let's go back to Shein as an example. In its website, the firm quite prominently showcases its "evoluSHEIN roadmap," with three pillars and nine priorities. It then highlights key initiatives. This includes mentioning the fact that the organization forged a partnership with the Apparel Impact Institute, underlining the fact that 14 of its plants are undergoing industrial waste recycling projects, showcasing that 10 supplier facilities are equipped with childcare centers, and reporting that 165 families have been supported with family assistance.[15]

Note how the clothier advertises the *existence* of such initiatives, rather than their results or progress. Even where it does publish myriad sustainability claims, the numbers are clearly unimpressive—given Shein's size.

Another classic corporate comms tactic deployed by Operators is communicating on safe ideas or themes without giving enough details and figures. Shein has, for example, sought favorable headlines by launching a peer-to-peer clothing reuse platform, "Shein exchange."

Shein also advances social claims that suggest it is democratizing fashion by making stylish garments available to low-income customers: "Making the beauty of fashion available to all." An alternative analysis advanced by other observers is that the firm is selling mass-produced clothing using low-wage labor, at the environmental cost of more than 16 million metric tons of CO_2 per year.[16]

Yet Shein will likely continue down its well-forged route. Operators are typically tireless lobbyists that use non-market strategies to curb existing regulations and prevent or weaken proposed ones. In 2024, for example, in the United States, Shein hired senator Marco Rubio's former chief of staff as a lobbyist, and in France, it hired Christophe Castagner, the former Minister of the Interior.[17] Its spending on lobbyists had risen to almost $4 million per year by 2024.[18]

Now let us examine Strivers' approach to corporate communications. Rather than highlighting initiatives, as Operators do, Strivers seek to communicate something more robust. They highlight *progress.*

Apple is a classic example of a Striver. Like most Strivers, it publishes weighty reports that outline progress toward its sustainability goals—Apple's sustainability report is actually called "Apple's Environmental *Progress* Report."[19] At first glance, such publications can look impressive. Yet upon closer examination, they can often rely on unambitious commitments, disclaimers, and favorable baselines. As such, the claims in Apple's Report might well be considered modest. Some 22% (less than a quarter) of materials shipped in its products were from recycled and renewable sources. It also boasts that more than 12 million devices have been sent to new owners for reuse in 2023. If this sounds like a lot, consider that there are 2.2 *billion* active Apple devices worldwide.[20] Recall the backlash the tech major received for its ad where Mother Nature—played by Hollywood actress Octavia Spencer—is seemingly happy with its sustainability claims, despite her barely interrogating them.[21]

Strivers' publications are often characterized by citing mandatory steps or basic regulatory compliance as achievements. There are cases where they do commit the firm to achieving measurable goals. But these targets are typically unrealistic and ultra long-term. Scratch below the surface, and Strivers rarely demonstrate meaningful progress against their targets. Take, for example, a global supplier to the construction industry. It has a published goal of becoming net zero in 2050—far in the future. Yet, based on current trends, the firm has little chance of achieving its objective. By its own figures, it reduced carbon emissions by a mere 1.1% per year between 2018 and 2023. Yet, its own objective is to increase that rate to 3% between 2023 and 2030, and it must achieve a further 11% reduction per year between 2030 and 2050 to meet its goals!

The final category of more traditional comms strategists are the Enthusiasts. Companies in this category use their comms to highlight *purpose*. They seek to demonstrate how the purpose and mission of a company or brand are related to SDG-level problems. To validate their claims, Enthusiasts frequently undergo governance changes that embed their sustainability credentials in the business.

Consider, for example, Danone, the French food corporation. Danone has become a B Corp, a global movement of companies committed to responsible social and environmental practice. It seeks—and wins—accreditation from a range of industry and sustainability bodies for delivering on its stated mission to bring healthy food to the masses. Like all Enthusiasts, it aims to lead—not follow—on sustainability. In 2020, Danone became the first publicly listed firm to become a Société à Mission—a French legal framework that obliges companies to integrate social and environmental goals into their business model.

Enthusiasts like Danone use a comprehensive, coherent, and consistent set of sustainability objectives. They endeavor to stay true to their word on sustainability. And because of that, their risk of greenwashing is lower.

Clean Winners corporate communication

Clean Winners eschew such a fragmented approach. Rather, they emphasize how enhanced sustainability fosters better performance.

Consider this key difference. Traditional sustainability strategies *highlight* various aspects of their sustainability activity in their corporate communication. By contrast, Clean Winners *integrate* sustainability in their general communication efforts, and they *modulate* the intensity of sustainability communication depending on the industry exposure and the message complexity.

INTEGRATION. Clean Winners' sustainability comms and business comms are integrated and intertwined. Sometimes, they use an "integrating device." For example, Schneider Electric—the energy management company from France—promotes EcoStruxure, a digital platform that helps its clients maximize energy efficiency throughout their premises. Such integrating devices help customers interlock better business performance (lower costs) with sustainability (reduced environmental impact). Schneider's approach to communications aligns with that dual-benefit approach: "Our mission is to be your partner for sustainability and energy efficiency," it says. Its products "drive sustainable financial performance." Sika, the Swiss specialty chemical manufacturer, is similarly resonant: "The company helps its customers build healthier and safer buildings and vehicles with a lower carbon footprint."

A second way Clean Winners integrate their communications efforts is by *emphasizing continuity.* Because sustainability initiatives are anchored in the firm's long-honed capabilities, the firm is merely "accelerating" objectives that it was already pursuing.

Rather than create myriad sustainability goals as an add-on, the focus is on how they are using sustainability to advance toward their long-standing mission.

Siemens, the German tech giant, excels here. "To *move faster,* we need to make adoption easier and scalable," according to its 2024 sustainability report. "We are strengthening our position as the world's leading technology company with unmatched capability to combine the real and digital worlds."

Finally, Clean Winners employ resonant communications. Their comms promote the benefits of sustainability *to the customer*: "Performance is the foundation for doing good," says Schneider in a promotional video.

For its part, Siemens communicates how sustainable solutions enhance customer value: "We develop scalable technologies that are easier to deploy and use. This involves doing things differently from the past, like developing eco-friendly products that solve common challenges shared by many customers."

MODULATION. Integration is not the only aspect of Clean Winners' communications. The company also pragmatically adjusts sustainability commu-

FIGURE 7-5

Modulating corporate sustainability communication

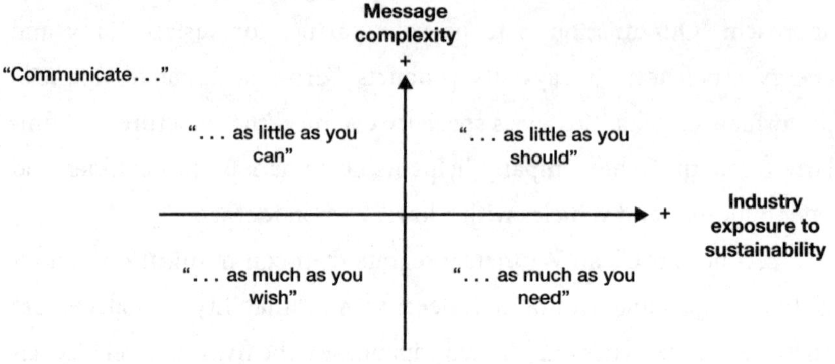

nication intensity based on two main considerations: industry exposure and message complexity (figure 7-5). In certain situations, firms may thus limit discussion of sustainability in their corporate communications—and it does not mean that they have "something to hide."

Some sectors face greater scrutiny around sustainability due to media attention, NGO actions, or past scandals, even if not fully justified. For instance, although the building and construction industry generates 40% of global carbon emissions,[22] it is often viewed positively for building essential infrastructure. As a result, construction firms might not feel pressured to communicate about sustainability. In contrast, aviation produces less than 3% of emissions,[23] but faces intense public criticism. Firms belonging to such sectors cannot afford to remain silent about its environmental impact.

The other aspect to consider is the complexity of the sustainability message. In some situations, information is straightforward to convey and visualize, allowing firms to communicate sustainability topics with relative ease. In other industries, however, messages may be more complex and require technical terminology or detailed analyses such as life-cycle assessments. In such cases, firms should carefully plan their communication strategies.

Exposure and complexity combined creates four different situations. Being a Clean Winner sometimes means keeping quiet about sustainability in corporate comms.

When you have a complex message in an unexposed industry, active sustainability-focused corporate comms is likely unwise (see top left of figure 7-5). Companies in unexposed industries face minimal external pressure to demonstrate their sustainability credentials to investors and stakeholders. Thus, there is little to be gained by communicating in this way. Instead, they should focus their messaging on commercial qualities, such as revenue, profit, and talent pool—and the quality of their products.

By contrast, in an exposed industry, it is crucial to highlight your sustainability credentials to investors—but you must proceed with extreme care (see top right of figure 7-5). Consider an airline that is developing sustainable aviation fuel (SAF) and more efficient airliners. These technologies are complex and tricky to explain. In this scenario, the airline's comms team must convey the benefits to stakeholders. Yet they must also be aware that talking imprecisely in an area that is exposed to the public glare leaves them prone to accusations of greenwashing. Proceed with caution.

When messages are clear and straightforward to convey, corporate comms becomes somewhat easier. Teams that have the luxury of a simple message in an unexposed industry can be vocal—they can communicate on sustainability as much as they like (see bottom left of graphic). When the claim is more complex, it pays to be conservative (see bottom right of graphic). Clean Winners in this space know to communicate deliberately and pragmatically on sustainability.

In all cases, organizations must—as always—make a full and frank assessment of their situation. Communications on sustainability—at the corporate or product-level—can provide a commercial tonic to a firm. But, as with so many facets of business strategy, it requires effective leadership—which we explore in the final chapter.

8

Leadership Enablement

Clean Winners Show the Way

Stephen, a senior executive known for his commitment to sustainability, remained unusually quiet after the CEO announced ambitious new sustainability goals. Colleagues were puzzled by his silence, prompting one to say, "You should be thrilled—we're ramping up again." Stephen replied with a wry smile, "It's sustainability, you have to be like a preacher at first. But then you must cease to preach. Will I know when to stop preaching sustainability?"

We have a saying at IMD: "In the end, it is all about leadership." This may refer to the fact that almost 40% of our colleagues are leadership professors, a high number. It also conveys our institutional belief that the "how" matters, enormously. Sustainability strategy is no exception, and we view effective leadership as the final key enabler.

Sustainability brings much for business leaders to ponder. It exists in a complex and varied regulatory landscape. It evokes reactions from activist investors, who prioritize shareholder value, and militant NGOs, who want nothing to do with profit. It divides customers into those who believe in it and those who are indifferent to it. It is easy to argue that

TABLE 8-1

Clean Winners: Championing Resonance

Leadership principles
Start as a sustainability activist, but quickly become a "grounded" actor
You don't need a sustainability strategy because sustainability is an enabler
Building a sustainability culture is unnecessary and a distraction; instead, be customer-centric
Don't be opportunistic with sustainability; instead strive for coherence
Put CSOs in a position of strength instead of "setting them up to fail"

the very existence of sustainability makes life more complicated for leaders. This is true—to an extent. However, leaders of Clean Winners exploit the opportunities from sustainability.

In this final chapter, we explore how leaders champion Resonance within their companies. We underline five principles that emerged in our research. Maybe Stephen was right to be worried . . . (see table 8-1). We then "put everything together" and illustrate these principles through an unexpected Resonator: Nespresso.

1. Start as a Sustainability Activist, but Quickly Become a "Grounded" Actor

In 2024, *Financial Times* associate editor Pilita Clark coined the term "Greenlash."[1] Her portmanteau of green and backlash captured the trend perfectly. There is no denying it. The sustainability journey is getting tougher. Major firms such as BP, Coca-Cola, Crocs, Nestlé, Nike, Shell, Tractor Supply, and Unilever have all rolled back sustainability commitments.[2]

To make sense of this, we asked dozens of leaders a simple question: "What percentage of your resources on sustainability are spent on meeting regulatory requirements?" The answer was typically 60–80%. To ensure our data was unbiased, we did some secondary research. We found an IBM study that showed spending on sustainability reporting exceeded spending on sustainability innovation by 43%. Only 31% of executives surveyed said they are incorporating sustainability data and insights into operational improvements to any great extent. A mere 14% said they do so similarly with innovation initiatives.[3] Clearly, the gravitational pull to be an Operator is strong.

To overcome this gravity, firms need leaders who are initially willing to behave like sustainability activists—green messiahs. Stefan Klebert, CEO of GEA, believed he needed to be like a preacher in order to build a sense of urgency in the firm. Prioritizing sustainability requires making trade-offs. It requires changing processes. If a leader is unwilling to be a powerful advocate of sustainability, the firm's employees will refuse to make those difficult trade-offs.[4]

The inspiration to become an advocate can come from different sources. Some have deep-rooted ethical and religious convictions. According to Paul Polman: "I first wanted to be a priest, then a doctor, but ended up in business and learned that I can help more people here to improve their lives."[5] Others' convictions are the result of a maturation process. Schneider Electric's Jean-Pascal Tricoire cites the fact that his grandfather was a farmer and that he witnessed firsthand social challenges, when he was managing the South African subsidiary of Schneider Electric, and environmental challenges, when he built the Chinese business for the energy management company.

For some, the inspiration came as an epiphany. "The Banega Swasth [Become Clean] campaign championed by the Indian Prime Minister became an inspiration for me and our team in India," revealed Fabrice Beaulieu, former chief marketing, sustainability, and corporate affairs officer at Reckitt. "That program dates to 2014. It was the first time we realized to which extent some of our brands could create positive impact.

Dettol is a leading disinfectant product. There was a natural fit with India's aspiration. . . . It was rather extraordinary because we had never thought of our brands as systematic enablers of social causes. This is when the penny dropped—and I became an advocate."

Some leaders converted their advocacy into a new vision that tied sustainability to innovation—e.g., Schneider Electric's EcoStruxure, GE's Ecoimagination, or Sumitomo Forestry's Life Cycle Carbon Minus House (a bold ambition to achieve a negative carbon footprint from construction to demolition by using superior wood).

This activist phase is crucial for kickstarting the sustainable transformation effort. But we believe that it must be short-lived. Leaders should quickly shed their activist role and become grounded in market reality. Otherwise, there is a danger that they will become Enthusiasts rather than Resonators.

One of the authors observed a top management meeting at a leading multinational company where the CEO was introducing new sustainability initiatives. When two senior country managers raised concerns about possible negative business impacts, they were sharply criticized. The lesson was clear to everyone: Market reality was taking a backseat, and the CEO had become an Enthusiast.

Becoming grounded in market reality means regularly communicating with those responsible for running company P&L statements. This is especially important in global companies where the impact of sustainability decisions made in global headquarters can sometimes be less obvious on the front lines.

A leader at a consumer packaged goods firm said that the company was initially focused on simply achieving sustainability targets. But according to him, this caused "a problem of diverging interests."

"P&L owners, for example, were against spending money [on sustainability] if they felt it was nonessential in their region," the leader added. "And then the marketing people felt they needed to use sustainability for brand creation. . . . We cannot force these things. With the new leadership, we are more connected to the markets and much better aligned in connecting sustainability to business value."

As we have learned, a key role for leaders is to steepen the innovation trajectory. Consider the case of buildings technology conglomerate Johnson Controls. It has been steadily shifting R&D resources toward sustainability innovation. In 2023, it put 90% of its R&D effort into sustainability innovation projects. The payoff is clear. Some 57% of the company's revenues now derive from its sustainability-related offerings.[6] From 2000 onward, its performance-contracting projects have directly reduced 39 million metric tons of carbon emissions and delivered long-term cost savings of over $8.4 billion.[7]

2. You Don't Need a Sustainability Strategy Because Sustainability Is an Enabler

Sustainability strategies are all the rage. Almost two-thirds (60%) of global companies had a sustainability strategy in 2024.[8] But you don't need a sustainability strategy to monetize sustainability.

One senior executive from a Fast Moving Consumer Goods (FMCG) firm recognized that his own firm had made this fundamental error. "Going back maybe five years, there was this hope that the consumer would be sufficiently worried about the future, and that she would fork out a bit more money for a product that is more sustainable," he recalled. "As you now know, this is, unfortunately, an extremely small niche."

Back at Reckitt, Beaulieu was similarly realistic. "Whatever the category, the majority of consumers will not want to pay a manufacturer to make the product more sustainable," he said. "Why would they? They think that's your problem. These are *your* sustainability objectives. So why should I fund them? If you give me a better product, then yes, I'll pay for it. Or at least I'll consider it."

Let's be clear. A sustainability *function* can be necessary in firms for several reasons. These include: the complexity of keeping abreast of and complying with fluctuating global regulations; departmental coordination; and educating employees about sustainability.

Yet a sustainability *strategy* is unnecessary. If the true role of sustainability is to increase customer value, then the value is already part of your "how to win" strategy choice. In this sense, sustainability is an enabler—plain and simple.

Beaulieu puts it well. "We have not developed a sustainability strategy," he said. "It's always about selling superior products. What we've done is added a sustainability lens to our brands."

Anurag Sharma, GM of Hilti Canada, subscribes to the same ethos. "Look at the pivot Hilti has made," he said. "It is to become bolder by being a customer's best partner for productivity, safety, *and* sustainability. These three elements do not operate separately—they intersect to become the right product."

Still, it remains all too easy for firms to become confused and make mistakes. Firms make top-down commitments at the corporate level, which executives are then expected to deliver on. Here, internal leadership is critical. "We have sustainability commitments at the top of the enterprise," said Beaulieu. "We make these real by connecting them to brand [or product] strategies."

The key here is that sustainability is linked with brand strategy—but not in a way that makes sustainability *the goal* (see figure 8-1). Rather, leaders like Beaulieu *add a sustainability lens*, which pushes the brand and product teams to holistically examine both the customer needs (job-to-be-done) and the unwanted outputs.

FIGURE 8-1

Linking sustainability commitments to strategy

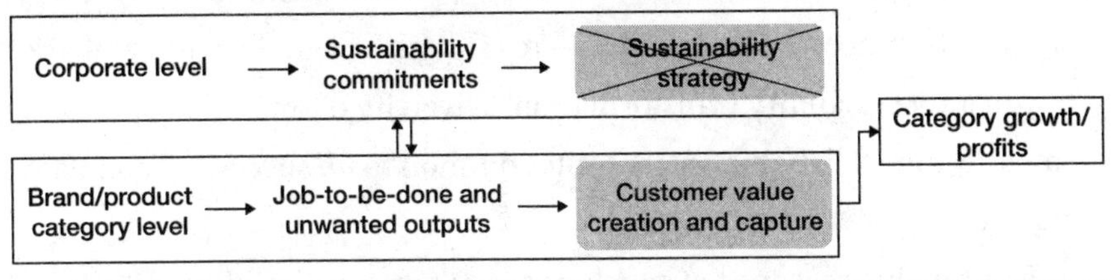

3. Building a Sustainability Culture Is a Distraction

Many analysts argue that firms must build a sustainability culture. The rationale for doing so is strong. The successful global MNCs of the twentieth century were founded before the age of sustainability. They lack an inherent sustainability culture. Thus, the thinking goes, they need a "deep cultural transformation" that puts sustainability at the center.[9]

A second, oft-cited, reason for developing a sustainability culture is the need for cohesive action. The thinking is that a "sustainability culture" fosters a collective mindset that influences all areas of an organization—from operations to decision-making. Thus, a sustainability-driven culture makes it easier to embed sustainability into every aspect of the business.

The third, commonly heard, reason is that sustainability actions in firms are often disjointed and are victims of organizational silos. A sustainability culture can overcome these problems, analysts argue.

The final reason relates to individual motivation. The idea is that a sustainability culture is essential because it enhances employee morale and attracts talent who value working for responsible organizations.[10] To implement sustainability in a meaningful manner, the thinking goes, firms must build a culture that encourages diverse opinions. They must also build cultures that are open, empathetic, and collaborative.[11]

Let's pause and think about this for a moment. Doesn't every organization need these qualities—regardless of whether it is embarking on a sustainability transformation? Diversity of opinions, openness, empathy and collaboration are traits common to *all* successful company cultures.

It is for this reason that much of the advice on "building a sustainability culture" has good intentions, but is ultimately impractical. Every leader we have worked with says that building the right culture is among the hardest tasks they encounter. Maintaining it is even more difficult. The problem, leaders report, is that they are bombarded with advice on building different cultures. A decade ago, they were told to build a digital culture. Then, they were asked to develop an agile culture. More recently, they became tasked with advancing a sustainability culture. Today, many leaders are being charged with creating an AI culture. These serial assignments are a distraction. They increase costs, add bureaucracy and a crazy number of meetings, and—crucially—reduce a firm's focus on serving their customers better than their competitors.

Our advice is simple—avoid being buffeted by ephemeral trends. Focus on the one truism in business—companies closest to customers win. A customer-centric culture is the only culture firms need. Successful firms have an enduring customer culture that concentrates on creating value for customers.

Behaviors are the foundation of such a culture. Firms that are customer-centric engage in three core behaviors. They generate market and customer insights quickly. They share those insights quickly within the organization. And they take quick action.[12] Several meta-analyses reveal that it is these three behaviors that enable commercial success. The key is to integrate sustainability into these three behaviors, so that it enhances a firm's customer value proposition.

4. Don't Be Opportunistic with Sustainability; Strive Instead for Coherence

Myriad firms' sustainability reports showcase their impact on a broad range of the United Nations Sustainable Development Goals (UN SDGs). It has become a badge of honor to demonstrate that a firm is doing good in many areas. For example, one company showed a link to twelve UN SDGs. Everything from creating new business opportunities to a conducive work environment were linked to specific SDGs. Yet strategy is about choices. Must a firm do good *everywhere*?

Many companies also engage in CSR initiatives that are unrelated to their business. Examples include a toilet paper manufacturer supporting the Amazon rainforest; a bank advocating reproductive rights; a trading firm promoting men's health issues; a furniture maker endorsing refugee support programs; an ice cream maker espousing social justice; and a shoemaker condemning plastics in the ocean. These are all laudable causes. And, in some cases, there may be good business logic in engaging in such programs—such as appeasing a local government. Yet, in most instances, these are merely opportunistic initiatives. They are perhaps the pet choice of a senior executive, or the result of a vote by employees on which projects to support, or just outright greenwashing.

Clean Winners take a more thoughtful approach. A senior executive outlined the shift within his company. "Instead of having businesses [brands] suggesting a variety of sustainability initiatives and then activating all that is required to reach certain sustainability KPIs, we now look at the initiatives to see whether they enhance the brand proposition," he said.

The key point here is that firms can use sustainability to enhance the brand proposition only where there is *coherence*—an authentic and logical linkage to a brand's value proposition. "Even though a brand or product category can impact multiple SDGs, we asked every brand to pick just one sustainability problem that has a clear link to the brand and that the R&D teams could solve through their expertise," said Beaulieu.

An exemplar from Beaulieu's firm is Harpic, a toilet cleaner in the Reckitt portfolio. Reckitt identified a direct linkage to UN SDG #6: "clean water and sanitation for all." Thus, it worked with communities in countries such as India to educate local people on how to improve accessibility to clean water.

Also at Reckitt, Vanish sells stain removers for clothes. It could have opted for a UN SDG such as climate action or gender equality. But the brand found a *direct* association with reducing clothing waste. It is innovating to help clothes last longer. Thus, Vanish aligned with SDG #12: "responsible consumption."

5. Put CSOs in a Position of Strength Instead of Setting Them Up to Fail

The job of a CSO has never been easy. They often suffer from role ambiguity. Many are given insufficient resources. Too few are handed the necessary power to do their jobs.[13] The truth is that many CSOs are in "stealth PR roles." Their primary responsibility is to tell the world about all the good a company is doing for its stakeholders.[14] Such roles are set up to fail.

Recently, many CSOs have become more directly involved in the business. They attend investor meetings. They help product managers identify trade-offs.[15] Yet these ostensibly enhanced roles are similarly set up to fail—because the key trade-offs are inadequately articulated. For example, should a company use fossil fuels for production to be market competitive or switch to green alternatives?

Some analysts suggest that the CSO has eight roles: regulatory compliance, ESG monitoring, managing sustainability projects, managing stakeholders, building sustainability capabilities, promoting culture change, scouting and experimenting through open innovation, and embedding sustainability into decision-making.[16] This is a comprehensive set of activities. Yet it lacks priorities, especially those focused on creating customer value.

The better approach is to use organizational design to enable CSO success. One method is to merge the CSO role with a functional role that focuses on customer value. The story of Sika, the chemical manufacturer, illustrates this well. The company's CEO, Thomas Hasler, had previously held the position of CTO (chief technology officer). Hasler knew how crucial product formulations and material choices were to making better and more efficient products. Thus, in 2021, he combined the firm's innovation and sustainability functions. CSO Patricia Heidtman oversees both product development and sustainability.

Consider, too, the case of renewable energy company Enel. It designed a new corporate unit called Innovability. The word "innovability" is a combination of "innovation" and "sustainability." As the name suggests, the unit combines the two critical functions.[17] This ensures that sustainability opportunities are explored seriously—but with commercial feasibility in mind.

Another strategy is to bring cross-functional teams together to address business issues. At Reckitt, Beaulieu would convene brand directors, R&D directors, and sustainability specialists to enhance customer value through sustainability.

Similarly, electrical engineering multinational ABB uses product development as a bridge between sustainability, engineering, and sales functions. A senior executive at the company noticed that company silos were making it difficult to leverage sustainability. "R&D was too much inside out and too technical," he said. "They prioritized performance gains but overengineered products. If you're a sustainability person, you would say, 'make the most efficient model.'

But somebody [else] in your organization is saying, 'I don't want it to double the cost.' So that's where you need the product management people to come in. Disjointed teams increase costs. So, Product Management connects the ideas from various functions to bring the most cost-effective development to the market."

Leadership Enablement at Nespresso

Many readers will wonder why Nespresso—whose parent company is Nestlé—qualifies as a Clean Winner. They have reason to be skeptical. The company's use of aluminum and plastics, which protect the coffee's flavor, have been panned by environmentalists as creating excess waste.[18] NGOs have also raised concerns about the efficacy and transparency of the firm's coffee capsule recycling programs.[19] Nespresso fits very well in the cell "High Industry Exposure" and "High Message Complexity" at the end of chapter 7. The general predicament in terms of corporate communication was "communicate as little as you should."

To combat some of this negativity, in late 2022, Nespresso reported that it had become carbon neutral. That was the same year that the firm was granted B Corp certification.[20] Yet neither its claimed carbon neutrality nor its B Corp status is sufficient reason to pick Nespresso as a Clean Winner. There is more to the story.

Nespresso's leaders exemplify many of the leadership principles we have highlighted, specifically in how they navigated the challenges of the company's sustainability journey.

Let's begin with the controversial capsules. Aluminum is infinitely recyclable. An independent study by the University of Quebec concluded that single-dose coffee capsules are less wasteful and more ecologically friendly than filtered and brewed coffee.[21]

Yet the consumer *image* of Nespresso pods was an ugly one. Customers and media viewed aluminum as resource wastage and questioned Nespresso's recycling rates.[22] The BBC reported the Quebec study's findings as an example of consumer cognitive biases.

"You have zero chance to be heard," admitted a senior leader. "You can argue [with consumers] that it's an emotional perception. And you might say, 'let's rationalize, let's explain, let's educate.' [But] they'll [still] think you're greenwashing."

Rather than fight a losing battle with consumers over the misconception that aluminum pods are unsustainable, Nespresso's leaders decided to combat an emotional perception with an "emotional proposition." Nespresso has launched in France and Switzerland compostable paper pods. "It changed the narrative," said one leader. "You get the chance to engage with journalists in a completely different way. We had positive articles in media that had been killing us for the last ten years. You're lovable again. Instead of telling people, "You're wrong about aluminum, we give consumers a choice." Nespresso's refurbished RELOVE machines add positivity to this conversation.

The company has invested CHF 1 billion into its Positive Cup sustainability initiative since 2014.[23] Much of it directed into improving farm practices.[24] What have farming practices got to do with Nespresso's core customer value proposition? The answer is: everything.

The story begins where every coffee bean begins—in the soil. "Nespresso stands for delivering unforgettable taste," an executive told us. "Taste starts with soil. If you're not approaching soil in a sustainable manner, then you're breaking your [taste] promise already. The reason to engage in sustainability is just to deliver on our promise."

As a Nespresso executive said: "Before talking about a coffee bean and a coffee tree, you create a taste through the way you manage your soil."

Nespresso's heavy investments into regenerative agriculture help preserve its core brand associations—taste, quality, and product availability.[25] Why product availability, you may ask?

Coffee futures hit their highest level in almost fifty years in November 2024. The prices of beans have nearly doubled since the beginning of the year. Much of the price increase has to do with poor weather conditions and EU's deforestation laws.[26] The expectation is that climate will continue to critically degrade coffee-growing areas, hampering coffee production.

Nespresso anticipated this a long time ago. Over the past twenty years, Nespresso has built *direct* relationships with over 150,000 farmers in eighteen countries. These direct relationships allow Nespresso to support farmers in regenerative agriculture and building supply chain resiliency. Today, 93% of its coffee beans are sustainably sourced.

Nespresso also launched its Reviving Origins initiative in 2014. Some coffee growing regions were afflicted by natural disasters and instability. Nespresso invested in helping farmers rebuild their farms in such conflict regions, like the Congo and Colombia. This improved farmer livelihoods. But it also revived unique origin coffee varieties from such regions—giving Nespresso a competitive edge.[27]

CONCLUSION

The Battle for Tomorrow

Clean Winners Must Win the Global Race

Netscape launched in 1994, followed by Internet Explorer in 1995. By 2000, computers were in most US homes and had spread globally. Investors, optimistic about the new market, heavily funded dot-com companies.

Dot-coms were changing the traditional paradigms of finance. Investors were discovering the network effects, and growth was receiving undue attention to the detriment of profit—soon dubbed a "quaint concept" by the *Wall Street Journal*.[1] "Grow fast or die" became the mantra. The NASDAQ composite index grew fivefold between 1996 and 2000, reaching an unheard price-earning ratio of forty-five.[2] At the time, it seemed that simply adding the ".com" suffix to your company name would be enough to go public and raise money.

In March 2000, however, the bubble exploded. Many dot-com companies failed or were acquired; larger companies, such as CISCO and Amazon, also lost substantial value. It took less than two years for the NASDAQ to go back to its pre-bubble level.

Why are we telling this story? We recognize that there are obvious differences, but we see a parallel between the dot-com bubble and what we call "the first wave of sustainability." This time, it is not growth, but sustainability that took center stage. When firms are guided by a specific question—"How can we become be more sustainable?"—when investing in sustainability initiatives, they de facto overlook the returns on those investments.

As we go to press, we see a correction that mimics the post-bubble times. Sustainability (or Green) fatigue is now increasing from all sides. A Deloitte report revealed that more citizens and customers are disengaging, possibly due to a lack of visible impact or frustration with greenwashing.[3] Major companies such as Coca-Cola, Chevron, HSBC or Unilever are reducing their sustainability commitments.[4] In January 2025, the Science Based Targets initiative (SBTi) removed 239 global companies, including Microsoft, Procter & Gamble, and Walmart, from its list due to missed climate submission deadlines.[5] Financial institutions such as BlackRock and Goldman Sachs are exiting climate-related initiatives, and investors are now withdrawing from ESG funds.[6] Last, organizations such as the World Economic Forum (WEF) and the Intergovernmental Panel on Climate Change (IPCC) face growing scrutiny.[7] Rough times for sustainability—or so it seems.

Now, the trillion-dollar question: Did the internet cease to exist after the crash? No. The dot-com boom was just not the way in which the internet would eventually flourish.

Here is our safe prediction: Will sustainability issues disappear given current greenlash? No. What we are witnessing is a painful, but probably needed, correction.

Let's be clear: The first wave of sustainability, with its Operators, Strivers, and Enthusiasts was most probably needed; "Nothing great has ever been accomplished without passion," said Georg Wilhelm Friedrich Hegel. That passion enabled sustainability to enter the corporate world, and to become a major area of interest. And rightfully so. But at one point, passion meets the reality of the world.

We believe that sustainable offerings that ask customers to accept lower value, worse performance, or reduced affordability are doomed to fail: While consumers might enjoy a short-term dopamine hit from feeling they are "saving the planet," in the medium-term such ideas are doomed. Companies that demand compromise from their own customers likely compromise their own chances of success. Unless sustainability enhances customer value, consumers will eventually tire of it and refuse to pay for it—even if they were once willing to in the past.

It's time to rethink sustainability, by looking at the world as it is, not as it should be. Call it "sustainability 2.0" if you wish. We refer to this new approach as "Resonance"—a clear strategy that ties sustainability directly to customer value and aligns it with business success and profitability. We identify three non-exclusive paths to Resonance and three supporting enablers. We show evidence that firms achieving Resonance succeed in the market with sustainability. They are the Clean Winners.

Customers will purchase more sustainable products where such products materially improve their lives. It is this opportunity—this encouraging truth—that inspired us. We realized that if we could change the thinking within the world's biggest firms, then creating "sustainable sustainability" would be possible.

Clean Winners has unearthed proven exemplars that show the way. Think back to Product Resonance, the first type of Resonance that we explored. Consider how Reckitt made a massive splash with its Finish dishwasher tablet. Don't tell customers they need to change their lives by expending more time and energy washing dishes with greener—but inferior—detergents. Instead, innovate to make both their lives, and that of the planet, easier. Finish is better than many of its competitors. It saves customers time, water, and thus money. And, because it reduces demand for a scarce resource, it also happens to be better for the planet.

Recall Michelin as well, one of the leading lights of Model Resonance. The French giant is a company that broke the mold by offering Tires as a Service to the haulers on a pay-per-use model. Technology is again key: Telematics and pressure sensors monitor the tires and the way the trucks are being driven in real-time. Through innovation, customers save money through longer-lasting tires and improved fuel efficiency. And Michelin has an incentive to make tires that last—they will be returned to Michelin for repair and maintenance. Less waste and more fuel efficiency. Everybody wins.

Those universal gains were delivered, too, by our strategic Resonators. Remember Mahindra Group's pivot from supplier of agricultural equipment to a new playing field: farming consultancy and management. Its visionary chairman, Anand Mahindra, realized that many Indian farmers were unable to afford Mahindra's high-tech machinery, so he pledged instead to build "a nation of champion farmers" in his native India, by offering them onsite expertise. Mahindra now educates farmers on new ways of growing crops to obtain better yields—using 13,000 single-acre plots to show how yields can be enhanced—and shows them that farming can be more efficient and planet-friendly when using the right technology and the right inputs in the right place at the right time. It's a business made more financially and environmentally sustainable through innovation.

The climate crisis—a global challenge as fierce and acute as a world war—can create the next innovation engine. With smart collective thinking, the need to protect scarce resources, reduce carbon emissions, and curb rising temperatures can turn entire economies into Clean Winners: Territories that, through invention and ideas, improve the human condition—creating lasting public value—while simultaneously protecting the planet from that which would otherwise destroy it.

Yet for that to happen, a war of ideas must first be won. The future of the Earth demands that Clean Winner thinking must overcome a well-meaning, but misguided, rival doctrine—the failed, morally charged, and unsustainable sustainability practices of the past.

Customers must no longer be told they are wrong to purchase so-called unsustainable goods and services. Instead, Clean Winners must show them that value, affordability, and performance can go hand-in-hand with sustainability. This book is a prospectus aiming to solve the environmental emergency with a powerful consumerism that works for people, profit, and planet.

On the individual, corporate, and national levels, *sustainable sustainability* requires great leaders that want, and are empowered, to lead that change. Leaders offering an answer that asks the public to improve one area of their lives (their environment) by impairing others (their wealth, family, or social lives) are in fact offering no answer at all. Humans rarely volunteer to be worse off. Rather, the course of human progress relies on a collective desire for each generation to be wealthier than the one before.

The stories in this book reveal Clean Winner thinking across manifold industries and numerous nations. They demonstrate that sustainable sustainability strategies that enhance customer value, rather than reduce it, are not only possible but—with intelligent design—even probable.

These ideas are an antidote to a credo that said to do good you likely have to do less well. Not only is that moral crusade ineffective, it is actively damaging. The planet will not prosper if its people fail to prosper as well.

Clean Winners think differently. They deliver sustainable sustainability to provide material benefit. They use sustainable technologies to improve the customer experience. They couple environmental efficiency with better performance. Their ideas must become principles for the next age.

NOTES

Introduction

1. All of these figures are taken from Unilever, *Annual Reports & Account 2010—Creating a Better Future Every Day*, accessed February 17, 2025, https://www.unilever.com/files/origin/55645ff8fe907166422f0d5db6ccb849f30c9348.pdf/unilever-ar10.pdf.

2. “Stock Price History for Unilever (UL),” CompaniesMarketCap, accessed February 17, 2025, https://companiesmarketcap.com/gbp/unilever/stock-price-history.

3. “Sustainability Ratings and Rankings,” Unilever, accessed July 29, 2024, https://www.unilever.com/sustainability/responsible-business/sustainability-ratings-and-rankings.

4. Bain & Company, *The Visionary CEO’s Guide to Sustainability 2024—How Leaders Can Meet the Moment with Pragmatism*, accessed February 17, 2025, https://www.bain.com/globalassets/noindex/2024/bain_report_the_visionary_ceos_guide_to_sustainability-2024.pdf.

5. CapGemini Research Institute, *Consumer Products and Retail—How Sustainability Is Fundamentally Changing Consumer Preferences*, accessed February 17, 2025, https://www.capgemini.com/wp-content/uploads/2020/07/20-06_9880_Sustainability-in-CPR_Final_Web-1.pdf.

6. “PwC’s Voice of the Consumer 2025—A New Recipe for the Food Industry,” PwC, June 10, 2025, https://www.pwc.com/gx/en/issues/c-suite-insights/voice-of-the-consumer-survey.html.

7. “Consumers Care About Sustainability—and Back It Up with Their Wallets,” McKinsey & Company, February 6, 2023, https://www.mckinsey.com/industries/consumer-packaged-goods/our-insights/consumers-care-about-sustainability-and-back-it-up-with-their-wallets.

8. “Unilever’s Purpose-Led Brands Outperform,” Unilever, July 17, 2019, https://www.petnology.com/online/news-detail/unilevers-purpose-led-sustainable-living-brands-outperform.

9. “Why Today’s Pricing Is Sabotaging Sustainability,” Kearney, September 11, 2020, https://www.kearney.com/industry/consumer-retail/article/-/insights/why-todays-pricing-is-sabotaging-sustainability.

10. Tjark Freundt, Cornelia Grossmann, Sascha Lehmann, and Yvonne Staack, “Talk Is Cheap: How Much Will Consumers Really Pay for Green Products?” McKinsey & Company, April 25, 2024, https://www.mckinsey.com/capabilities/growth-marketing-and-sales/our-insights/talk-is-cheap-how-much-will-consumers-really-pay-for-green-products.

11. "Attitude-Behavior Gap Report," Zalando, April 20, 2021, https://corporate.zalando.com/en/our-impact/sustainability/sustainability-reports/attitude-behavior-gap-report#exploring-the-attitude-behavior-gap.

12. Theodore Levitt, *The Marketing Imagination* (New York: The Free Press, 1983), 127.

13. Owen Walker, "The Long and Short of the Quarterly Report Controversy," *Financial Times*, July 1, 2018, https://www.ft.com/content/e61046bc-7a2e-11e8-8e67-1e1a0846c475.

14. Unilever, *Unilever's Sustainable Living Plan*, accessed on July 25, 2024, https://www.unilever.com/files/92ui5egz/production/9752ff2d82b8afabb507eb92c47b5dad795801d5.pdf.

15. Unilever, *Unilever's Sustainable Living Plan*.

16. "Unilever's Purpose-Led Brands Outperform."

17. The Unilever Group COS Personal Products, *DJSI Industry Leader Report | 2020*, accessed July 29, 2024, https://www.unilever.com/files/c6e49d6d-e580-44bf-92ce-3e6ef0a376de/acrobat-document.pdf.

18. "Sustainability Ratings and Rankings."

19. Unilever, *Delivering Sustainable Business Performance—Unilever Annual Report and Accounts 2022*, accessed July 29, 2024, https://www.unilever.com/files/92ui5egz/production/0daddecec3fdde4d47d907689fe19e040aab9c58.pdf.

20. Yearly evolution of Unilever share price (US$; start of the year): 2021, –13%; 2022, –6%; 2023, –4%; 2024, +18%. Data from Yahoo! Finance, https://finance.yahoo.com/.

21. Harriet Agnew, "Unilever Has 'Lost the Plot by Fixating on Sustainability,' Says Terry Smith," *Financial Times*, January 11, 2022, https://www.ft.com/content/7aa44a9a-7fec-4850-8edb-63feee1b837b.

22. Richa Naidu and Radhika Anilkumar, "Unilever to Cut a Third of Office Jobs in Europe," *Financial Times*, July 12, 2024, https://www.ft.com/content/2f6afe99-2dc3-4ae2-81a5-35585deec0e9.

23. Joel Makower, "Why Unilever's Downshift on Sustainability Is Good News," Trellis, November 6, 2023, https://trellis.net/article/unilevers-downshift-sustainability.

24. Unilever, *Climate Transition Action Plan*, March 22, 2021, https://assets.unilever.com/files/92ui5egz/production/bbe89d14aa9e0121dd3a2b9721bbfd3bef57b8d3.pdf/unilever-climate-transition-action-plan-19032021.pdf.

25. Makower, "Why Unilever's Downshift on Sustainability Is Good News."

26. David Gelles, "Billionaire No More: Patagonia Founder Gives Away the Company," *New York Times*, September 14, 2022, https://www.nytimes.com/2022/09/14/climate/patagonia-climate-philanthropy-chouinard.html.

27. Timo Busch and Gunnar Friede, "The Robustness of the Corporate Social and Financial Performance Relation: A Second-Order Meta-Analysis," *Corporate Social Responsibility and Environmental Management* 25, no. 4 (2018): 583–608.

28. "Unilever's Purpose-Led Brands Outperform."

29. "Consumers Care About Sustainability—and Back It Up with Their Wallets."

30. Tensie Whelan and Carly Fink, "The Comprehensive Business Case for Sustainability," hbr.org, October 21, 2016, https://hbr.org/2016/10/the-comprehensive-business-case-for-sustainability.

31. Katie McQuater, "Unilever Shifts Sustainability Focus and Appoints Growth and Marketing Chief," Research Live, October 30, 2023, https://www.research-live

.com/article/news/unilever-shifts-sustainability-focus-and-appoints-growth--marketing-chief/id/5118773.

32. McQuater, "Unilever Shifts Sustainability Focus and Appoints Growth and Marketing Chief."

Chapter 1

1. "Beyond Checking the Box," IBM, February 27, 2024, https://www.ibm.com/thought-leadership/institute-business-value/en-us/report/sustainability-business-value.

2. Gayatri Suroyo, Stefanno Sulaiman, and Ananda Teresia, "Indonesia Accuses EU of 'Regulatory Imperialism' with Deforestation Law," Reuters, June 8, 2023, https://www.reuters.com/business/environment/indonesia-accuses-eu-regulatory-imperialism-with-deforestation-law-2023-06-08/.

3. Katherine Masters, "How Shein Outgrew Zara and H&M and Pioneered Fast-Fashion 2.0," Reuters, December 13, 2023, https://www.reuters.com/business/retail-consumer/how-shein-outgrew-zara-hm-pioneered-fast-fashion-20-2023-12-13.

4. "Shein's Annual Profit Down By More than a Third, FT Reports," Reuters, February 23, 2025, https://www.reuters.com/business/retail-consumer/sheins-profits-drop-by-more-than-third-2024-ft-reports-2025-02-23.

5. David Curry, "Shein Revenues and Usage Statistics," Business of Apps, updated January 22, 2025, https://www.businessofapps.com/data/shein-statistics.

6. Marianna Chairez, Veronica Shedd, and Athina Azevedo, "Shein; The Exploration of Their Clothing Cycle & the Raw Materials That Craft It," Design Life-Cycle, March 16, 2023, https://www.designlife-cycle.com/shein-clothing. See also Dilys Williams, "Shein: The Unacceptable Face of Throwaway Fashion," *Guardian*, April 10, 2022, https://www.theguardian.com/fashion/2022/apr/10/shein-the-unacceptable-face-of-throwaway-fast-fashion.

7. Shein Group, *Accelerating the Revolution—2022 Sustainability & Social Impact Report*, accessed July 25, 2024, https://www.sheingroup.com/wp-content/uploads/2024/05/2022_SHEIN_SustainabilitySocialImpactReport-1.pdf; Sachi Kitajima Mulkey, "Shein Is Officially the Biggest Polluter in Fast Fashion," *Yale Climate Connections*, September 19, 2024, https://yaleclimateconnections.org/2024/09/shein-is-officially-the-biggest-polluter-in-fast-fashion-ai-is-making-things-worse.

8. "How China's Shein Became a Fast-Fashion Giant," *Economic Times*, November 28, 2023, https://economictimes.indiatimes.com/tech/technology/how-chinas-shein-became-a-fast-fashion-giant/articleshow/105548640.cms?from=mdr.

9. Laura Onita and Eleanor Olcott, "Shein to Launch €200Mn Fund to Tackle Fashion Waste as It Awaits IPO Approval," *Financial Times*, July 9, 2024, https://www.ft.com/content/de96ce29-dceb-40a5-9253-e53a736886bb.

10. Bob Koigi, "Gillette Launches New Line of Products That Are Kind to Skin and Planet," *Marketing Report*, February 9, 2021, https://marketingreport.one/brand-and-sustainability/gillette-launches-new-line-of-products-that-are-kind-to-skin-and-planet.html.

11. Grant Davidson, "Gillette Planet KIND; Branding a Movement," Davidson Branding, August 6, 2021, https://davidsonbranding.com.au/gillette-planet-kind-branding-a-movement; Koigi, "Gillette Launches a New Line of Products That Are Kind to Skin and the Planet."

12. Federica Laricchia, "Apple's Revenue 2000–2024, by Operating Segment (in Billion U.S. Dollars)," Statistica, June 23, 2025, https://www.statista.com/statistics/265125/total-net-sales-of-apple-since-2004.

13. Apple, *2024 Environmental Progress Report*, accessed July 25, 2024, https://www.apple.com/environment/pdf/Apple_Environmental_Progress_Report_2024.pdf.

14. Mehul Reuben Das, "Apple Again Accused of Planned Obsolescence, to Be Investigated by French Regulators," *Firstpost*, May 16, 2023, https://www.firstpost.com/world/apple-again-accused-of-planned-obsolescence-to-be-investigated-by-french-regulators-12601802.html.

15. "iPhone Repair & Service," Apple, accessed July 29, 2024, https://support.apple.com/iphone/repair.

16. Sandra Laville, "Amazon and Apple 'Not Playing Their Part' in Tackling Electronic Waste," *Guardian*, November 26, 2020, https://www.theguardian.com/technology/2020/nov/26/amazon-and-apple-not-playing-their-part-in-tackling-electronic-waste.

17. Ariel Zilber, "Apple Climate Film with Octavia Spencer Is Slammed: 'This Is Greenwashing'," *New York Post*, September 14, 2023, https://nypost.com/2023/09/14/apple-video-on-climate-change-featuring-octavia-spencer-is-slammed; Gordon Young, "What Mother Nature Would Really Make of Apple and the iPhone 15," *The Drum*, September 14, 2023, https://www.thedrum.com/opinion/2023/09/14/what-mother-nature-would-really-make-apple-and-the-iphone-15.

18. Justine Calma, "Apple's First Carbon Neutral Products Are a Red Herring," *The Verge*, September 12, 2023, https://www.theverge.com/23870317/apples-watch-series-9-carbon-neutral-climate-goal.

19. Apple, *Product Environmental Report: Apple Watch Series 9—Carbon Neutral*, September 12, 2023, https://www.apple.com/environment/pdf/products/watch/Carbon_Neutral_Apple_Watch_Series_9_PER_Sept2023.pdf.

20. Kenza Bryan, "Apple's 'Carbon Neutral' Come Under Scrutiny," *Financial Times*, October 23, 2023, https://www.ft.com/content/90392004-97e0-4444-a5cd-82220fe52510.

21. Rebecca Henderson, *Reimagining Capitalism in a World on Fire* (New York: PublicAffairs, 2020).

22. Edelman, "Alan Jope on Purpose and the Role of Business," posted January 22, 2019, YouTube video, 01:17, https://www.youtube.com/watch?v=FIWviHlgP7w.

23. Preserve (website), accessed September 3, 2025, https://www.preserve.eco.

24. "Founding Story," Preserve, accessed August 20, 2024, https://www.preserve.eco/pages/founding-story.

25. Sinan Erzurumlu, "Preserve: Growing a Sustainable Consumer Goods Company" (Babson Park, MA: Babson College, 2018).

26. Erzurumlu, "Preserve."

27. Preserve, "B Corp Certification," accessed September 3, 2025, https://www.preserve.eco/pages/bcorp-certification.

28. Preserve, "Preserve's Investor Webinar (Recording)," posted June 23, 2023, YouTube video, 0:41:51, https://www.youtube.com/watch?v=CXJJQieSn6E.

29. Preserve, *Preserve—Sustainable Food Service Products*, accessed February 18, 2025, https://cdn.shopify.com/s/files/1/0058/2854/2552/files/Preserve-FoodService-Catalog-Digital.pdf?v=1693498656.

30. "Beyond Checking the Box: How to Create Business Value With Embedded Sustainability," *IBM Business Insights*, February 27, 2024, https://www.ibm.com/thought-leadership/institute-business-value/en-us/report/sustainability-business-value.

31. "Bringing Centrifuges up to Speed with Sustainability," GEA, August 12, 2024, https://www.gea.com/en/stories/bringing-centrifuges-up-to-speed-sustainability.

32. "Bringing Centrifuges up to Speed with Sustainability."

33. "EcoStruxure Platform," Schneider Electric, accessed August 20, 2024, https://www.se.com/in/en/work/campaign/innovation/platform.

34. Frédéric Dalsace, "Schneider Electric: Becoming the World Leader in Sustainability" (Lausanne: IMD, 2022).

35. Schneider Electric, *2023 Sustainable Development Report*, accessed February 18, 2025, https://www.se.com/ww/en/assets/564/document/466155/2023-sustainability-report.pdf; Schneider Electric, "Schneider Electric Boosts Its Innovation Ecosystem with 'Schneider Electric Ventures' to Identify, Nurture and Support Bold Ideas," press release, November 13, 2018, https://www.prnewswire.com/news-releases/schneider-electric-boosts-its-innovation-ecosystem-with-schneider-electric-ventures-to-identify-nurture-and-support-bold-ideas-300749390.html.

Chapter 2

1. Not all RTCs are sustainability benefits. For example, customers who want to buy local products to help the local economy may do so without thinking about sustainability.

2. Charitable donations might present as an exception to this rule. There are many examples of people making anonymous donations with no personal benefit for the exclusive purpose of improving the planet's social or environmental conditions. Yet these are *not* an exception to the rule—because donations are not, by definition, purchases.

3. Connor Morpurgo, "Electric Vehicle Sales in Germany Plummet," *Euro Weekly News*, January 9, 2025, https://euroweeklynews.com/2025/01/09/electric-vehicle-sales-in-germany-plummet-as-pressure-mounts-on-nations-economy.

4. See, for example, Deborah J. Webb, Lois A. Mohr, and Katherine E. Harris, "A Re-Examination of Socially Responsible Consumption and Its Measurement," *Journal of Business Research* 61, no. 2 (2008): 91–98; or, Magdalena Öberseder, Bodo Schlegelmilch, Patrick Murphy, and Verena Gruber, "Consumers' Perceptions of Corporate Social Responsibility: Scale Development and Validation," *Journal of Business Ethics* 124, no. 1 (2014): 101–115.

5. Michael G. Luchs, Rebecca W. Naylor, Julie R. Irwin, and Rajagopal Raghunathan, "The Sustainability Liability: Potential Negative Effects of Ethicality on Product Preference," *Journal of Marketing* 74, no. 5 (2010): 18–31.

6. Ying-Ching Lin and Chiu-chi Angela Chang, "Double Standard: The Role of Environmental Consciousness in Green Product Usage," *Journal of Marketing* 76, no. 5 (2012): 125–134.

7. Aaron R. Brough, James E. B. Wilkie, Jingjing Ma, Mathew S. Isaac, and David Gal, "Is Eco-Friendly Unmanly? The Green-Feminine Stereotype and Its Effect on Sustainable Consumption," *Journal of Consumer Research* 43, no. 4 (December 2016): 567–582.

8. "Why We Are Not on All Lists of Ethical Chocolate Brands," Tony's Chocolonely, February 13, 2021, https://tonyschocolonely.com/blogs/news/why-we-are-not-on-all-lists-of-ethical-chocolate-brands.

9. "La Roche-Posay Cardboard Tube," Albéa Group, June 3, 2020, https://www.albea-group.com/article/la-roche-posay-cardboard-tube.

10. Ioannis Ioannou, George Kassinis, and Giorgos Papagiannakis, "How Greenwashing Affects the Bottom Line," hbr.org, July 21, 2022, https://hbr.org/2022/07/how-greenwashing-affects-the-bottom-line.

11. NYU Stern, *Sustainable Market Share Index*, updated April 2024, https://www.stern.nyu.edu/sites/default/files/2024-05/2024%20CSB%20Report%20for%20website.pdf.

12. "Why Today's Pricing Is Sabotaging Sustainability," Kearney, September 11, 2020, https://www.kearney.com/industry/consumer-retail/article/-/insights/why-todays-pricing-is-sabotaging-sustainability.

13. "Who We Are," East-West Seed, accessed September 17, 2025, https://www.eastwestseed.com/about-us/.

14. "Beyond Checking the Box: How to Create Business Value With Embedded Sustainability," *IBM Business Insights*, February 27, 2024, https://www.ibm.com/thought-leadership/institute-business-value/en-us/report/sustainability-business-value.

15. "Empowering Customers with Resource-Efficient Solutions," GEA, accessed September 3, 2015, https://www.gea.com/en/sustainability/add-better-ecolabel.

16. "Empowering Customers with Resource-Efficient Solutions."

17. Robert G. Eccles and George Serafeim, "The Performance Frontier: Innovating for a Sustainable Strategy," hbr.org, May 2013, https://hbr.org/2013/05/the-performance-frontier-innovating-for-a-sustainable-strategy.

18. Pan Kwan Yuk, "US Retail's Multibillion-Dollar Returns Problem," *Financial Times*, December 26, 2024, https://www.ft.com/content/0fc7e452-3664-435b-b5d4-68529bce1df3.

19. "About Us," Horizon Pulp & Paper, accessed September 3, 2025, https://horizon.ee/who-are-we.

20. "Our Customization Process," OCP Group, accessed September 3, 2025, https://www.ocpgroup.ma/customization-process.

21. "Our Customization Process."

Chapter 3

1. We recognize, however, that not all RTCs are sustainability benefits. For example, buying local products to help the local economy.

2. Maersk, "Maersk to Deploy First Large Methanol-Enabled Vessel on Asia—Europe Trade Lane," press release, December 7, 2023, https://www.maersk.com/news/articles/2023/12/07/maersk-to-deploy-first-large-methanol-enabled-vessel-on-asia-europe-trade-lane.

3. Tim Hornyak, "Methanol-Fueled Ships: Testing of an ME-LGIM Engine in Korea," MAN Energy Solutions, accessed September 3, 2025, https://www.man-es.com/discover/methanol-fueled-ships

4. Technically, this cost is called the marginal abatement cost (https://en.wikipedia.org/wiki/Marginal_abatement_cost); for a global review, see Tomas Nauclér and Per-Anders Enkvist, *Pathways to a Low-Carbon Economy—Version 2 of*

the Global Greenhouse Gas Abatement Cost Curve, McKinsey & Company, 2009, https://www.mckinsey.com/capabilities/sustainability/our-insights/pathways-to-a-low-carbon-economy; or Jinggang Guo and Jeffrey P. Prestemon, "The Marginal Cost of Carbon Emissions Abatement Across Sectors," *Applied Economics* (March 2025).

5. As we will see below, the mere mention of the use of organic or green ingredients may change customers' perceptions—even if the product is as effective as the regular version (see chapter 2 regarding sustainability liability).

6. Mike Botan, "Electric Motorcycle Blues / LiveWire Tanks—Again," Adventure Rider, October 27, 2024, https://www.advrider.com/livewire-tanks-again.

7. Harley Davinson, *2023 Annual Report*, February 23, 2024, https://investor.harley-davidson.com/financials/quarterly-results/default.aspx.

8. Botan, "Electric Motorcycle Blues."

9. The phenomenon known as "loss aversion" will make the switch from the traditional to the sustainable offer less attractive in the case of Mixed Dissonance. Research has shown that the subjective value of losses outweighs the subjective value of equivalent gains ("losses loom larger than gains"). For a recent review, see Daniel Kahneman and Amos Tversky, "Prospect Theory: An Analysis of Decision Under Risk," *Econometrica* 47, no. 2 (1979): 263–291; or Lukasz Walasek, Timothy L. Mullett, and Neil Stewart, "A Meta-Analysis of Loss Aversion in Risky Contexts," *Journal of Economic Psychology* 103 (August 2024).

10. Jonah Malin, "How Oatly Permanently Changed the Way We Drink Milk," *Medium*, June 7, 2020, https://medium.com/@jonahmalin/how-oatley-permanently-changed-the-way-we-drink-milk-d219861cc38c.

11. Armand V. Cardello, Fabien Llobell, Davide Giacalone, Christina M. Roigard, and Sara R. Jaeger, "Plant-Based Alternatives vs. Dairy Milk: Consumer Segments and Their Sensory, Emotional, Cognitive and Situational Use Responses to Tasted Products," *Food Quality and Preference* 100 (September 2022); Sally Wadyka, "We Tried 3 Plant-Based Milks That Claim to Mimic Dairy Milk," *Consumer Reports*, September 19, 2022, https://www.consumerreports.org/health/milk-milk-alternatives/plant-based-milks-that-claim-to-mimic-dairy-milk-a1132416550/.

12. Malin, "How Oatly Permanently Changed the Way We Drink Milk."

13. Oatley, "Oatly Reports Third Quarter 2024 Financial Results," news release, November 7, 2024, https://investors.oatly.com/news-releases/news-release-details/oatly-reports-third-quarter-2024-financial-results.

14. "The Evolution of the Prius," Toyota, August 4, 2017, https://global.toyota/cn/prius20th/evolution.

15. "Road Test: 1997 Toyota Prius," Greenfleet, accessed September 3, 2025, https://greenfleet.net/road-tests/18012017/road-test-toyota-prius-1997.

16. David Bach and David Bruce Allen, "What Every CEO Needs to Know About *Non*market Strategy," *MIT Sloan Management Review*, April 2010, https://sloanreview.mit.edu/article/what-every-ceo-needs-to-know-about-nonmarket-strategy/.

17. Mack Hogan, "Toyota's Hybrids Dominated Last Year," Inside EVs, January 31, 2025, https://insideevs.com/news/749260/toyota-hyrids-global-sales-2024.

18. Michael Wayland, "GM, Ford Report Best Annual U.S. Sales Since 2019 as Auto Recovery Continues," CNBC, January 3, 2025, https://www.cnbc.com/2025/01/03/ford-2024-us-sales.html.

19. "Make Clothes Last Twice as Long with Half the Environmental Impact," Electrolux Group, accessed September 3, 2025, https://www.electroluxgroup.com

/sustainabilityreports/2021/key-priorities-and-progress-2021/our-nine-goals/better-living/make-clothes-last-twice-as-long-with-half-the-environmental-impact.

20. “New QMAX Thermally Enhanced Core,” CURRIES, accessed September 3, 2025, https://www.curries.com/en/customer-resources/news/2023/new-qmax-thermally-enhanced-core.

21. “DURABRIC—A Game Changer in Constuction,” DURABRIC, accessed November 3, 2025, https://www.durabric.com/.

22. “Fatality Facts 2023,” Insurance Institute for Highway Safety (IIHS), July 2025, https://www.iihs.org/topics/fatality-statistics/detail/state-by-state.

23. National Highway Traffic Safety Administration, “NHTSA: Traffic Crashes Cost America $340 Billion in 2019,” press release, January 10, 2023, https://www.nhtsa.gov/press-releases/traffic-crashes-cost-america-billions-2019.

24. Alltech, “Alltech and Agolin Partner to Provide Eco-Friendly Nutrition Solutions for Supporting Cattle Production and Sustainability Goals,” press release, May 4, 2023, https://www.alltech.com/ae-en/features-press-release/alltech-and-agolin-partner-provide-eco-friendly-nutrition-solutions.

25. Sika Group, “Sika Posts Record Sales of CHF 11.24 Billion in 2023—Growth of 7.1% in CHF,” press release, January 10, 2024, https://www.sika.com/en/media/media-releases/2024/sika-posts-record-sales-in-2023.html.

26. “Sika Launches the SPM Framework,” Sika, accessed September 3, 2025 https://www.sika.com/en/media/insights/sikanews/sustainability-portfolio-management.html.

27. Sika, *Sika Sustainability Portfolio Management (SPM) Methodology*, accessed October 7, 2024, https://www.sika.com/dam/dms/corporate/media/glo-ar-2023-spm-methodology.pdf.

28. “Sika Launches the SPM Framework.”

29. Ben Fox Rubin and Suruchi Kapur-Gomes, “India Spent $30 Billion to Fix Its Broken Sanitation. It Ended Up with More Problems,“ CNET, September 11, 2020, https://www.cnet.com/culture/india-spent-30-billion-to-fix-its-broken-sanitation-it-ended-up-with-more-problems.

30. “Powering the Future of Youth Sport,” Nike, accessed September 3, 2025, https://www.nike.com/future-of-sport.

31. Pamela N. Danziger, “Nike Declares 2019 Its Year for Women,” *Forbes*, March 1, 2019, https://www.forbes.com/sites/pamdanziger/2019/03/01/nike-the-worlds-most-valuable-fashion-brand-declares-2019-its-year-for-women.

32. Danziger, “Nike Declares 2019 Its Year for Women.”

Chapter 4

1. Tanya Mohn, “Americans Are Driving More, and That Means More Risk,” *Forbes*, February 27, 2019, https://www.forbes.com/sites/tanyamohn/2019/02/27/americans-are-driving-more-and-that-means-more-risk.

2. The average US car capacity comes from the Bureau of Transportation Statistics and the *EPA Automotive Trends Report*; the number of persons per car is from the University of Michigan Center for Sustainable Systems’ Personal Transportation Factsheet (https://css.umich.edu/sites/default/files/2023-10/Personal%20Transportation_CSS01-07.pdf, accessed June 28, 2025). Interesting statistics to note: In the United States, vehicles now average 4,300 pounds (2 tons), and they carry on average 280 pounds of human flesh (1.5 human beings, weighing 185 pounds each).

See "Body Measurements," National Center for Health Statistics, accessed June 28, 2025, https://www.cdc.gov/nchs/fastats/body-measurements.htm.

3. Jose A. Guajardo, Morris A. Cohen, Sang-Hyun Kim, and Serguei Netessine, "Impact of Performance-Based Contracting on Product Reliability: An Empirical Analysis," *Management Science* 58, no. 5 (May 2012): 961–979.

4. Wolfgang Ulaga, Frédéric Dalsace, and Chloé Renault, "Business Model Innovation: Michelin Fleet Solutions—From Selling Tires to Selling Kilometers," case study IMD-5-0793, June 2013, https://www.imd.org/research-knowledge/marketing/case-studies/business-model-innovation-michelin-fleet-solutions-from-selling-tires-to-selling-kilometers.

5. Rent the Runway, accessed May 2023, https://www.renttherunway.com.

6. Circle Economy, *Circularity Gap Report 2025*, accessed June 29, 2025, https://global.circularity-gap.world.

7. "Eliminating Waste," Zero Waste World, accessed November 3, 2025, https://www.brambles.com/zero-waste-world/eliminating-waste.html.

8. "Fries to Miles—Circularity Partnership," Neste, accessed November 2, 2025, https://www.neste.com/news-and-insights/circular-economy fries-miles-circularity-partnership.

9. Emmanuel Oyedeji, "CHART: Apple Led the Refurbished Smartphone Market by Nearly 50% in 2022," *Techloy*, April 26, 2023, https://www.techloy.com/apple-refurbished-iphones-grew-16-percent-yoy-globally-in-2022/.

10. "Furniture as a Service," Ahrend, accessed November 4, 2025, https://www.ahrend.com/en/services/furniture-as-a-service.

11. Mehdi Nezami, Stefan Worm, and Robert W. Palmatier, "Disentangling the Effect of Services on B2B Firm Value: Trade-Offs of Sales, Profits, and Earnings Volatility," *International Journal of Research in Marketing* 35, no. 2 (June 2018): 205–223; Ashkan Faramarzi, Stefan Worm, and Wolfgang Ulaga, "Service Strategy's Effect on Firm Performance: A Meta-Analysis of the Servitization Literature," *Journal of the Academy of Marketing Science* 52, no. 4 (July 2024): 1018–1044; Konstantinos Ladas, Stylianos Kavadias, and Christoph Loch, "Product Selling vs. Pay-Per-Use Service: A Strategic Analysis of Competing Business Models," *Management Science* 68, no. 7 (July 2022): 4964–4982.

12. Stefan Worm, Sundar Bharadwaj, Wolfgang Ulaga, and Werner Reinartz, "When and Why Do Customer Solutions Pay Off in Business Markets?" *Journal of the Academy of Marketing Science* 45, no. 4 (July 2017): 490–512.

13. Guajardo et al., "Impact of Performance-Based Contracting on Product Reliability."

14. Ulaga, Dalsace, and Renault, "Michelin Fleet Solutions."

15. Renewcell, "Re:NewCell Decides to File for Bankruptcy," February 24, 2024, https://www.renewcell.com/en/renewcell-decides-to-file-for-bankruptcy/.

16. McKinsey & Company, "Entrepreneurship at All Levels: How Decathlon Innovates for the Future," April 26, 2023, https://www.mckinsey.com/capabilities/people-and-organizational-performance/our-insights/entrepreneurship-at-all-levels-how-decathlon-innovates-for-the-future.

Chapter 5

1. A.G. Lafley and Roger L. Martin, *Playing to Win: How Strategy Really Works* (Boston: Harvard Business Review Press, 2013).

2. "How Western Ireland's Sligo Hospital Has Saved Money and Solved Its Delta T Problem with Intelligent Solutions from Grundfos," Grundfos, accessed September 3, 2025, https://www.grundfos.com/about-us/cases/how-western-irelands-sligo-hospital-has-saved-money.

3. H. Igor Ansoff, "Strategies for Diversification," *Harvard Business Review* (1957): 113–124.

4. Iberdrola, "Iberdrola and Volvo Car España Commit to Sustainable Mobility," news release, January 27, 2022, https://www.iberdrola.com/press-room/news/detail/iberdrola-volvo-car-espana-commit-sustainable-mobility.

5. Shantanu Bhattacharya and Lipika Bhattacharya, "NIO: Battling Tesla with Battery as a Service," Singapore Management University, December 12, 2021, https://ink.library.smu.edu.sg/cases_coll_all/386.

6. "What's New with NIO in June 2025," NIO, July 1, 2025, https://www.nio.com/news/20250702001.

7. "What's New with NIO in June 2025."

8. "Goal 3: Ensure Healthy Lives and Promote Well-Being for All at All Ages," United Nations, accessed September 3, 2025, https://www.un.org/sustainable development/health.

9. "Healthy Habits," Lysol, accessed September 3, 2025, https://www.lysol.com/here-for-healthy-schools/healthy-habits.

10. "F-150 Lightning," Ford, accessed July 3, 2025, https://www.ford.com/trucks/f150-lightning.

11. "Performance," Ford, accessed July 3, 2025, https://www.ford.com/trucks/f150-lightning/performance.

12. "Performance," Ford.

13. "Ford Home Backup Power," Sunrun, accessed July 3, 2025, https://www.sunrun.com/ev-charging/ford-f150-lightning.

14. "Ford Home Backup Power."

15. "Supporting HEINEKEN's Net-Zero Ambition," Siemens, accessed September 3, 2025, https://www.siemens.com/global/en/products/buildings/references/heineken.html.

16. "Supporting HEINEKEN's Net-Zero Ambition."

17. "The Crit'Air Anti-Pollution Vehicle Sticker," France.fr, March 15, 2024, https://www.france.fr/en/article/crit-air-anti-pollution-vehicle-sticker.

18. "Our Purpose and Our Values Engage Us," Michelin, accessed October 24, 2024, https://www.michelin.com/en/group/purpose-values.

19. "Sustainable Logistics—Watèa by Michelin Sets Out to Conquer Hydrogen Mobility," Michelin, December 15, 2023, https://news.michelin.co.uk/articles/sustainable-logistics-watea-by-michelin-sets-out-to-conquer-hydrogen-mobility.

20. "Watèa by Michelin Launches Hydrogen Mobility Solution," Mobility Portal Europe, January 3, 2024, https://mobilityportal.eu/watea-by-michelin-hydrogen-mobility-solution/.

21. AAA Automotive, "True Cost of Electric Vehicles," AAA, accessed October 22, 2024, https://www.aaa.com/autorepair/articles/true-cost-of-ev.

22. Mahindra & Mahindra Ltd., *Integrated Annual Report 2023–24*, accessed October 17, 2024, https://www.mahindra.com/annual-report-FY2024/94/index.html.

23. Mahindra, "Mahindra Rolls Out Krish-e Centres in Maharastra," press release, October 2, 2020, https://www.mahindra.com/news-room/press-release/en/mahindra-rolls-out-krish-e-centres-in-maharashtra.

24. Murali Gopalan, "M&M's Krish-e Has Redefined the Art of Bonding with Farmers," *Auto Car Professional*, May 18, 2022, https://www.autocarpro.in/feature/mm-krishe-has-redefined-the-art-of-bonding-with-farmers-81774.

25. Ketan Thakkar, "Mahindra & Mahindra Eyes $200 Million Gross Merchandise Value from Farm Services," *The Economic Times*, October 5, 2022, https://economictimes.indiatimes.com/news/economy/agriculture/mm-eyes-200m-gross-merchandise-value-from-farm-services/articleshow/94651612.cms?from=mdr.

26. Richemont, *Executive Summary—Non-Financial Report 2025*, accessed July 3, 2025, https://www.richemont.com/media/1t4fcbmh/richemont-executive-summary-2025.pdf.

27. Alana Pipe and Nate Rattner, "How DeepSeek's Lower-Power, Less-Data Model Stacks Up," *Wall Street Journal*, February 16, 2025, https://www.wsj.com/tech/ai/deepseek-ai-how-it-works-725cb464?st=PYTuNx.

28. Hubert Joly, Nitin Nohria, and Emilie Billaud, "Michelin in Motion: Putting Purpose to Work," Harvard Business School Case 324-127, April 2024, https://www.hbs.edu/faculty/Pages/item.aspx?num=65893.

Chapter 6

1. Steven Gonzalez Monserrate, "The Staggering Ecological Impacts of Computation and the Cloud," *MIT Press Reader*, February 22, 2022, https://thereader.mitpress.mit.edu/the-staggering-ecological-impacts-of-computation-and-the-cloud.

2. Tammana Joon, "Data Centres in Ireland—Public Policy" PublicPolicy.ie, October 1, 2024, https://publicpolicy.ie/papers/data-centres-in-ireland.

3. Julia Binder and Michael Wade, "Digital Sustainability for a Better Future," *Stanford Social Innovation Review* (Winter 2024): 52–60.

4. PDD Holdings, "Pinduoduo Announces First Quarter 2022 Unaudited Financial Results," news release, May 27, 2022, https://investor.pddholdings.com/news-releases/news-release-details/pinduoduo-announces-first-quarter-2022-unaudited-financial/.

5. Yihan Ma, "Monthly Active Users of Mobile Shopping App Pinduoduo in China from 4th Quarter 2021 to 4th Quarter 2023 (in Millions)," Statista, June 30, 2024, https://www.statista.com/statistics/1399757/china-monthly-active-users-of-pinduoduo-app.

6. Feng Zhu, Krishna G. Palepu, Bonnie Yining Cao, and Dawn H. Lau, "Pinduoduo," Harvard Business School Case 620-040, September 2019 (revised November 2019), https://www.hbs.edu/faculty/Pages/item.aspx?num=56853.

7. Zhu et al., "Pinduoduo."

8. Pinduoduo, "Pinduoduo Expands Efforts to Bring Farmers Online, Promotes Smart Agriculture to Boost Productivity," press release, July 15, 2022, https://www.fooddive.com/press-release/20220715-pinduoduo-steps-up-agriculture-digital-inclusion-efforts.

9. Food and Agriculture Organization of the United Nations, "China's Pinduoduo Wins 2022 FAO Innovation Award," news release, June 12, 2022, https://www.fao.org/newsroom/detail/china-s-pinduoduo-wins-2022-fao-innovation-award.

10. "Investor Relations," John Deere, accessed October 29, 2024, https://investor.deere.com/home/default.aspx.

11. "Investor Relations."

12. John Deere, "See & Spray Customers See 59% Average Herbicide Savings in 2024," news release, September 28, 2024, https://www.deere.com/en/news/all-news/see-spray-herbicide-savings.

13. John Deere, "John Deere Acquires Smart Apply," news release, July 14, 2023, https://www.deere.com/en/news/all-news/john-deere-acquires-smart-apply.

14. John Deere, "John Deere Acquires Smart Apply."

15. Erick Burgueño Salas, "Revenue of Johnson Controls International from the Financial Year 2022 to 2024, by Segment (in Billion U.S. Dollars)," Statista, July 23, 2025, https://www.statista.com/statistics/199732/global-sales-of-johnson-controls-inc-since-2001.

16. Siew Kien Sia, Alvin Ng, and Ronald Hee, "Towards a Net Zero Future: The Digital Transformation of Johnson Controls for Sustainability," August 14, 2022, https://store.hbr.org/product/towards-a-net-zero-future-the-digital-transformation-of-johnson-controls-for-sustainability/NTU335?srsltid=AfmBOoqpcmJTnarzDNvr-hrts8Xbf_ybN4A1yzvAvE9y7voLLWb2IWh.

17. "OpenBlue," Johnson Controls, accessed October 24, 2024, https://www.johnsoncontrols.com/openblue.

18. "Blueprint of the Future for Smart, Sustainable Buildings," Johnson Controls, February 22, 2021, https://www.johnsoncontrols.com/insights/2021/featured-story/blueprint-of-the-future-for-smart-sustainable-buildings.

19. "Sustainability—Reports & Policies," Johnson Controls, accessed September 3, 2025, https://www.johnsoncontrols.com/corporate-sustainability/reporting-and-policies.

20. Wolfgang Ulaga, Frédéric Dalsace, and Chloé Renault, "Business Model Innovation: Michelin Fleet Solutions—From Selling Tires to Selling Kilometers," case study IMD-5-0793, June 2013, https://www.imd.org/research-knowledge/marketing/case-studies/business-model-innovation-michelin-fleet-solutions-from-selling-tires-to-selling-kilometers/.

21. "M-PESA," Vodafone, accessed August 16, 2024, https://www.vodafone.com/about-vodafone/what-we-do/m-pesa.

22. "Developers," M-PESA Africa, accessed September 3, 1015, https://www.m-pesa.africa/partners-developers.

23. "About Us," M-PESA Africa, accessed September 3, 2025, https://www.m-pesa.africa/about-us.

24. "About Us."

25. "M-PESA."

26. "M-Shwari," NCBA Group, accessed August 23, 2024, https://ke.ncbagroup.com/m-shwari.

27. "M-Shwari FAQs—Safaricom," Safaricom, June 30, 2021 (last updated September 22, 2023), https://www.safaricom.co.ke/media-center-landing/frequently-asked-questions/m-shwari-faqs-safaricom.

28. "Driven by Purpose: 15 Years of M-Pesa's Evolution," McKinsey & Company, June 29, 2022, https://www.mckinsey.com/industries/financial-services/our-insights/driven-by-purpose-15-years-of-m-pesas-evolution.

29. Murali Gopalan, "M&M's Krish-e Has Redefined the Art of Bonding with Farmers," *Auto Car Professional*, May 18, 2022, https://www.autocarpro.in/feature/mm-krishe-has-redefined-the-art-of-bonding-with-farmers-81774.

30. Mahindra, "Krish-e Launches IoT Based Smart Kit for Farm Equipment," press release, March 30, 2023, https://www.mahindra.com/news-room/press-release/krishe-launches-iot-based-smart-kit-for-farm-equipment.

31. Joe Panettieri, "E13: Johnson Controls VP & CTO Vijay Sankaran Describes Smart Buildings of the Future." Sustainable Tech Partner, March 20, 2024, https://sustainabletechpartner.com/podcast/e13-johnson-controls-vp-cto-vijay-sankaran-describes-smart-buildings-of-the-future.

32. "Factory Fresh," *Economist*, June 9, 2016. https://www.economist.com/technology-quarterly/2016/06/09/factory-fresh.

33. Lora Kolodny, "Deere Is Paying Over $300 Million for a Start-up That Makes 'See-and-Spray.' Robots," CNBC, September 6, 2017, https://www.cnbc.com/2017/09/06/deere-is-acquiring-blue-river-technology-for-305-million.html.

34. Bernard Marr, "The Amazing Ways John Deere Uses AI and Machine Vision to Help Feed 10 Billion People," *Forbes*, March 15, 2019, https://www.forbes.com/sites/bernardmarr/2019/03/15/the-amazing-ways-john-deere-uses-ai-and-machine-vision-to-help-feed-10-billion-people/?sh=56b96d02ae93.

35. John Deere, "John Deere's 2023 Business Impact Report Highlights Progress & Commitment to Sustainability Through Innovation," news release, January 23, 2024, https://www.deere.com/en/news/all-news/2023-business-impact-report.

36. "Investor Relations," Honeywell, accessed October 29, 2024, https://investor.honeywell.com.

37. Darius Adamczyk, "The Chair of Honeywell on Bringing an Industrial Business into the Digital Age," *Harvard Business Review*, March–April 2024, https://hbr.org/2024/03/the-chair-of-honeywell-on-bringing-an-industrial-business-into-the-digital-age.

38. "Presentations," Honeywell International Inc., accessed September 3, 2025, https://honeywell.gcs-web.com/events-and-presentations/presentations.

39. "Driven by Purpose."

40. Matthew Gault and Jason Koebler, "John Deere Hit with Class Action Lawsuit for Alleged Tractor Repair Monopoly," *VICE*, January 13, 2022, https://www.vice.com/en/article/john-deere-hit-with-class-action-lawsuit-for-alleged-tractor-repair-monopoly.

41. Richard Currie, "John Deere Signs Right to Repair Agreement with US Ag Lobbyists," *The Register*, January 9, 2023, https://www.theregister.com/2023/01/09/john_deere_repair_mou.

Chapter 7

1. J. G. Navarro, "Marketing in the United States—Statistics & Facts," Statista, February 28, 2025, https://www.statista.com/topics/8972/marketing-in-the-united-states.

2. Stefan Michel and Lisa S. Duke, *Real Impact Marketing*, 3rd ed. (Zurich: Business School Press, 2022).

3. In the remainder of this chapter, we will use the term "greenwashing" as a shortcut for "green- and social-washing."

4. Robyn Blakeman, *Integrated Marketing Communication*, 4th ed. (Lanham, MD: Rowman & Littlefield, 2023).

5. Richard E. Petty and John T. Cacioppo, "The Elaboration Likelihood Model of Persuasion," *Advances in Experimental Social Psychology* 19 (December 1986): 123–205. There is actually a continuum along these two strategies. For a recent review: Mukta Srivastava and Gordhan K. Saini, "A Bibliometric Analysis of the Elaboration Likelihood Model (EM)," *Journal of Consumer Marketing* 39, no. 7 (2022): 726–743.

6. Google Cloud, *CEOs Are Ready to Fund a Sustainability Transformation*, accessed February 13, 2025, https://www.gstatic.com/gumdrop/sustainability/google-cloud-cxo-sustainability-survey-final.pdf.

7. European Commission, *Environmental Claims in the EU—Inventory and Reliability Assessment—Final Report*, 2020, https://op.europa.eu/en/publication-detail/-/publication/f7c4cb8b-f877-11ee-a251-01aa75ed71a1/language-en.

8. For definitions of greenwashing—and discussions about the phenomenon—see Magali A. Delmas and Vanessa Cuerel Burbano, "The Drivers of Greenwashing," *California Management Review* 54, no. 1 (November 2011): 64–87; Thomas P. Lyon and A. Wren Montgomery, "The Means and End of Greenwash," *Organization & Environment* 28, no. 2 (June 2015): 223–249; Peter Seele and Lucia Gatti, "Greenwashing Revisited: In Search of a Typology and Accusation-Based Definition Incorporating Legitimacy Strategies," *Business Strategy and the Environment* 26, no. 2 (February 2017): 239–252; Esben Rahbek Gjerdrum Pedersen and Kirsti Reitan Andersen, "Greenwashing: A Broken Business Model," *Journal of Business Models* 11, no. 2 (August 2023): 11–24.

9. Delmas and Burbano, "The Drivers of Greenwashing."

10. "Huge Support for EU Law to Make Companies Accountable for the Climate Crisis," European Coalition for Corporate Justice, April 12, 2023, https://corporatejustice.org/news/huge-support-to-make-companies-accountable-for-climate-crisis.

11. "Attitoon Casual Minimalist Vintage Car Print Loose Round Neck Short Sleeve T-Shirt for Women," Shein, accessed December 12, 2024, https://us.shein.com/goods-p-40665123.html.

12. Sheila A. Millar, Jean-Cyril Walker, and Anushka N. Rahman, "Keurig Agrees to Pay $10 Million to Settle Class Action Over Charges of Misleading Recyclable Claims," *National Law Review*, March 1, 2022, https://natlawreview.com/article/keurig-agrees-to-pay-10-million-to-settle-class-action-over-charges-misleading.

13. Annika Harris, "Editor's Pick: Dove Refillable Deodorant Means Less Guilt, Same Efficacy," *Uptown*, January 22, 2021, https://www.uptownmagazine.com/style/editor-s-pick-dove-refillable-deodorant-means-less-guilt-same-efficacy; Dove US, "Dove Refillable Deodorant: Sustainable, Aluminum-Free, & Kind to Skin," posted January 4, 2021, YouTube video, 0:00:56, https://www.youtube.com/watch?v=BaAM4esd564.

14. Rajeev Jayaswal and Rezaul H. Laskar, "In India's FTA Talks with EU, Sustainability a Key Issue," *Hindustan Times*, August 26, 2024, https://www.hindustantimes.com/india-news/in-india-fta-talks-with-eu-sustainability-a-key-issue-101724628137631.html; Nicolas Köhler-Suzuki, "India and the European Union in 2030," Jacques Delors Institute, June 29, 2023, https://institutdelors.eu/en/publications/india-and-the-european-union-in-2030.

15. "Our Impact," Shein, accessed January 2025, https://www.sheingroup.com/our-impact.

16. Sachi Kitajima Mulkey, "Shein Is Officially the Biggest Polluter in Fast Fashion," *Yale Climate Connections*, September 19, 2024, https://yaleclimateconnections.org/2024/09/shein-is-officially-the-biggest-polluter-in-fast-fashion-ai-is-making-things-worse.

17. Caitlin Oprysko, "Former Rubio Chief Lobbying for Shein," *Politico*, April 25, 2024; Juliette Garnier, "La nomination de Christophe Castaner chez Shein indigne les professionnels français de la mode," *Le Monde*, January 14, 2025.

18. Caitlin Oprysko, "Shein Drops Its Outside Lobbyists," *Politico*, January 8, 2025.

19. Emphasis ours.

20. Backlinko Team, "Apple Statistics—Users, Devices, and Revenue," Backlinko, March 31, 2025, https://backlinko.com/apple-statistics.

21. Tom Corfman, "How Apple Missed the Mark with Octavia Spencer Ad," Rogan Consulting Group, September 25, 2023, https://raganconsulting.com/apple-miss-with-octavia-spencer-mother-nature-ad.

22. Christiana Hageneder, "Buildings and Construction: A Sleeping Giant for Climate Action," International Institute for Sustainable Development, January 28, 2020, https://www.iisd.org/articles/buildings-construction-sleeping-giant-climate.

23. Hannah Ritchie, "What Share of Global CO_2 Emissions Come from Aviation?" Our World in Data, April 8, 2024, https://ourworldindata.org/global-aviation-emissions.

Chapter 8

1. Pilita Clark, "Year in a Word: Greenlash," *Financial Times*, December 27, 2024, https://www.ft.com/content/0f72b2b4-e6cd-4372-9191-adce668bf2fb.

2. Kenneth P. Pucker, "Environmental Sustainability Companies Are Scaling Back Sustainability Pledges. Here's What They Should Do Instead," hbr.org, August 20, 2024, https://hbr.org/2024/08/companies-are-scaling-back-sustainability-pledges-heres-what-they-should-do-instead.

3. IBM, "IBM Study: Sustainability Remains a Business Imperative, But Current Approaches Are Falling Short," news release, February 28, 2024, https://newsroom.ibm.com/2024-02-28-IBM-Study-Sustainability-Remains-a-Business-Imperative,-But-Current-Approaches-are-Falling-Short.

4. Daniel C. Esty and Andrew S. Winston, *Green to Gold: How Smart Companies Use Environmental Strategy to Innovate, Create Value, and Build Competitive Advantage* (Hoboken, NJ: Wiley, 2009).

5. Paul Polman's 2014 interview with *Het Financieele Dagblad*, quoted in "Paul Polman Launches Sustainability Consulting Firm Imagine," Consultancy.eu, July 17, 2019, https://www.consultancy.eu/news/3027/paul-polman-launches-sustainability-consulting-firm-imagine.

6. Johnson Controls, *2024 Sustainability Report—Smart, Healthy, Sustainable Tomorrows*, April 22, 2024, https://www.johnsoncontrols.com/-/media/project/jci-global/johnson-controls/us-region/united-states-johnson-controls/corporate-sustainability/reporting-and-policies/documents/2024-sustainability-report.pdf.

7. Johnson Controls, *2024 Sustainability Report*.

8. Euromonitor International, "Three in Five Companies Implemented a Sustainability Strategy in 2024: Euromonitor International," press release, September 11, 2024, https://www.euromonitor.com/press/press-releases/september-2024/three-in-five-companies-implemented-a-sustainability-strategy-in-2024-euromonitor-international.

9. Elisa Farri, Paolo Cervini, and Gabriele Rosani, "How Sustainability Efforts Fall Apart," hbr.org, September 26, 2022, https://hbr.org/2022/09/how-sustainability-efforts-fall-apart.

10. PwC, *The Future of Work: A Journey to 2022*, accessed September 5, 2025, https://www.pwc.com/ee/et/publications/pub/future-of-work-report.pdf.

11. Farri, Cervini, and Rosani, "How Sustainability Efforts Fall Apart."

12. Ajay K. Kohli and Bernard J. Jaworski, "Market Orientation: The Construct, Research Propositions, and Managerial Implications," *Journal of Marketing* 54, no. 2 (April 1990): 1–18.

13. Robert G. Eccles and Alison Taylor, "The Evolving Role of Chief Sustainability Officers," *Harvard Business Review*, July–August 2023, https://hbr.org/2023/07/the-evolving-role-of-chief-sustainability-officers.

14. Eccles and Taylor, "The Evolving Role of Chief Sustainability Officers."

15. Eccles and Taylor, "The Evolving Role of Chief Sustainability Officers."

16. Elisa Farri, Paolo Cervini, and Gabriele Rosani, "The 8 Responsibilities of Chief Sustainability Officers," hbr.org, March 2, 2023, https://hbr.org/2023/03/the-8-responsibilities-of-chief-sustainability-officers.

17. Farri, Cervini, and Rosani, "How Sustainability Efforts Fall Apart."

18. "Coffee Pod Carbon Footprint Better for Planet than Filtered Brew," *BBC*, January 19, 2023, https://www.bbc.com/news/world-us-canada-64293750.

19. Elham Shirin, "Coffee Capsules: Brewing Up an (In)convenient Storm of Waste," *Mongabay*, December 20, 2022, https://news.mongabay.com/2022/12/coffee-capsules-brewing-up-an-inconvenient-storm-of-waste.

20. Clara Ludmir, "Nespresso Launches Its First Paper-Based Compostable Capsules," *Forbes*, September 13, 2023, https://www.forbes.com/sites/claraludmir/2023/09/13/nespresso-launches-its-pilot-of-home-compostable-capsules.

21. Luciano Rodrigues Viana, Charles Marty, Jean-François Boucher, and Pierre-Luc Dessureault, "Here's How Your Cup of Coffee Contributes to Climate Change," *The Conversation*, January 5, 2023, https://theconversation.com/here's-how-your-cup-of-coffee-contributes-to-climate-change-196648.

22. Ed Cumming, "How Nespresso's Coffee Revolution Got Ground Down," *Guardian*, July 14, 2020, https://www.theguardian.com/food/2020/jul/14/nespresso-coffee-capsule-pods-branding-clooney-nestle-recycling-environment.

23. Nespresso, *The Positive Cup—2023 Progress*, July 4, 2024, https://nestle-nespresso.com/sites/site.prod.nestle-nespresso.com/files/ nespresso_esg_the_positive_cup_2023_progress_document.pdf.

24. Kamran Kashani and Goutam Challagalla, "Nespresso: Strategy Reset for Growth—The Youth Market," IMD, October 2023, https://www.imd.org/research-knowledge/marketing/case-studies/nespresso-strategy-reset-for-growth-the-youth-market.

25. Santiago Gowland, "Towards the Regeneration of Coffee Farming," Nespresso, May 2022, https://www.sustainability.nespresso.com/regenerative-agriculture/regeneration-coffee-farming.

26. Susannah Savage, "Coffee Futures Hit 47-Year High on Global Supply and EU Law Fears," *Financial Times*, November 27, 2024, https://www.ft.com/content/02ed448b-7205-40c9-b4fd-2e56b8b1e4db.

27. Jérôme Perez, "Reviving Origins," Nespresso, April 2025, https://www.sustainability.nespresso.com/communities/reviving-origins.

Conclusion

1. Bernard Wysocki, "Companies Chose to Rethink a Quaint Concept: Profits," *Wall Street Journal*, May 19, 1999, https://www.wsj.com/articles/SB9270768713268007.

2. Preston Teeter and Jorgen Sandberg, "Cracking the Enigma of Asset Bubbles with Narratives," *Strategic Organization* 15, no. 1 (2017): 91–99.

3. Deloitte, "Cost and Sustainability Fatigue Stifle Consumers' Efforts to Adopt More Sustainable Lifestyles," October 27, 2024, https://www.deloitte.com/uk/en/about/press-room/cost-and-sustainability-fatigue-stifle-consumers-efforts-to-adopt-more-sustainable-lifestyles.html.

4. Marissa Heffernan, "Coca-Cola 'Evolves' Sustainability Goals, Timelines," *Plastics Recycling Update*, December 4, 2024; Walter Janberg, "Chevron Cuts Low-Carbon Investments Amid Financial Pressures," Report Linker, https://www.reportlinker.com/article/9575; Simon Jessop and Tommy Reggiori Wilkes, "HSBC Delays Net-Zero Emissions Target by 20 Years," Reuters, February 19, 2025, https://www.reuters.com/sustainability/hsbc-pushes-back-climate-emissions-target-review-policies-2025-02-19/; Rob Davies, "Unilever to Scale Back Environmental and Social Pledges," *Guardian*, April 19, 2024.

5. James Darley, "Why SBTi Has Delisted More Than 200 High Profile Companies," *Sustainability*, January 17, 2025, https://sustainabilitymag.com/articles/why-sbti-has-delisted-more-than-200-high-profile-companies.

6. Michael Posner, "How BlackRock Abandoned Social and Environmental Engagement," *Forbes*, September 12, 2024; Saptakee S, "Why Did Goldman Sachs Exit the Net-Zero Banking Alliance?" CarbonCredits.Com, December 10, 2024, https://carboncredits.com/why-did-goldman-sachs-exit-the-net-zero-banking-alliance.

7. Lauren Hirsch and Andrew Ross Sorkin, "A Vibe Shift at Davos," *New York Times*, January 18, 2025, https://www.nytimes.com/2025/01/18/business/dealbook/a-vibe-shift-at-davos.html; "'Building Trust' Key to Solving Climate Crisis, Cop30 President Tells RFI," *RFI*, April 25, 2025, https://www.rfi.fr/en/environment/20250425-building-trust-key-to-solving-climate-crisis-cop30-president-tells-rfi.

INDEX

Note: Page numbers followed by *f* and *t* refer to figures and tables, respectively. Those followed by n refer to notes, with note number.

ACKNOWLEDGMENTS

This book is a genuinely collaborative work—to the point that we would be hard-pressed to tell who wrote what.

The project began one day in fall 2020, when Goutam came to Frédéric's office to share his thinking in what was then a new area of interest for him: sustainability. Frédéric couldn't answer the questions that Goutam raised about a topic he thought he knew. This laid the groundwork for our research collaboration.

We noticed that something was odd in the field of sustainability: Executives complained about customers not following through on their stated intentions to buy sustainable products (what has been known as the "sustainability say-do gap"). Being both trained in marketing, we knew that blaming the customers could not be the answer. We decided to dig deeper. Our joint efforts led to the publication of two *Harvard Business Review* articles, and, ultimately to *Clean Winners*.

This book could not have existed without frequent interaction with company executives, and IMD provided us with unparalleled access to major companies. Work with firms like ABB, Atlas Copco, Hilti, Michelin, Nestlé, OCP, Reckitt, Schneider-Electric, Siemens, and Tetra Pak, among many others, shaped our thinking. And while it is difficult to single out individuals who assisted us along the way, we would particularly like to thank Matthias Altendorf, Fabrice Beaulieu, Patricia Heidtman, Pierre-Martin Huet, Bernad Meunier, Eva Riesenhuber, Anna Sjörén, Nadine Sterley, Sofia Svingby, and Gilles Vermot-Desroche.

As learning is a continuous process, we are constantly refining our ideas and discovering new ways to help firms make sustainability "resonate" with their strategy. IMD now offers a thriving suite of open programs in the field, including the Executive Master in Sustainable Business Transformation, which participants describe as "transformative." We specifically created an open program called Integrating Sustainability into Strategy, which expands on ideas from *Clean Winners*—and the program's participants help us shape our thinking further.

Writing a book when agendas are full is a formidable task. We would like to thank David Bach and Jean-François Manzoni, IMD's present and past presidents, for continuously encouraging us throughout this process. Frédéric still remembers Jean-François' piece of advice: "Drop your other projects, Frédéric, and tell us what both of you need to get *Clean Winners* done." Both Seán Meehan and Stefan Michel, IMD's faculty deans, played a key role in the process, and Delia Fischer, IMD's chief communication officer, was instrumental in helping with communications.

A special thanks goes to the Dentsu Group for having provided invaluable research support. Dentsu Group CEO Hiroshi Igarashi makes it a point to meet with Goutam every year to learn about his research and to support him. Dentsu Group executives Yoko Fukuyama, Hitoshi Hamaguchi, and Keita Kimura have been most helpful in knowledge dissemination.

From every angle you look, our collaboration with Harvard Business Review Press has been a stellar one. Gardiner Morse, an HBR contributing editor, is a sharp mind. He guided our paths toward the publication of our articles, and he encouraged us to think about the best positioning for this book. Executive Editor Jeff Kehoe master-minded the project and skillfully shepherded us, two rookies in the book-writing craft. If you liked *Clean Winners*, it is because Jeff transformed awkward manuscript chapters into a solid book. Our thanks also go to Angela Piliouras for her careful work on our manuscript.

This book would not have been possible if we hadn't taken time away from our families during countless evenings, weekends, and holidays. Goutam is very grateful to Madhavi, his spouse, for her patience, encouragement, and for making sacrifices to ensure he could achieve what he wanted. He also feels fortunate that Ayana, his daughter, is an independent child, which allowed him to spend time on researching the book. Frédéric wants to deeply thank Eliane, his wonderful partner, for her love, comprehension, and patience, and his children and quasi-children Ségolène, Baudouin, Graciane, Edouard, Olivier, Ella, and Basil, for putting up with all of this. Four amazing grandchildren were born during the process: Ombeline, Louis, Maximilien, and Isaure. May this book make a minuscule contribution to a more sustainable world, for them and for all!

ABOUT THE AUTHORS

GOUTAM CHALLAGALLA is Dentsu Group Chair in Strategy and Marketing at IMD. His research focuses on how digital technologies, AI, and sustainability concerns are impacting companies' business strategies and approaches to strategy and marketing.

Goutam is the director of the Advanced Management Program and the Strategy Governance for Boards program, and is co-director of the Integrating Sustainability into Strategy program.

He has led programs on strategy and marketing issues for clients from a wide range of B2B and B2C industries, including AT&T, Beiersdorf, Cargill, Caterpillar, GEA, Grundfos, Kone, Nestlé, Novo Nordisk, Pfizer, Reckitt, DNB Bank, TBC Group, and Zurich Insurance Group.

His research has been published in top strategy, marketing, and management journals. He is a winner of the Maynard Award (2015) for the overall best paper in the *Journal of Marketing*. He has published articles on sustainability and AI in *Harvard Business Review*. His latest article, "Stop Running So Many AI Pilots" (*HBR*, November–December 2025), advocates a narrow and deep approach to implementing AI. Another article (with Frédéric Dalsace), "How to Market Sustainable Products," was included in *HBR's 10 Must Reads 2025*.

Goutam has authored many case studies. His case study "Nespresso: Strategy Reset for Growth" (with Kamran Kashani) won the Overall category at The Case Centre Awards and Competitions 2025. Another case, "Has Nike Lost Its Stride?" (with Ivy Buche), is a John Molson MBA International Case Competition award winner.

Before joining IMD in 2015, Goutam worked for twenty years as a professor at the Georgia Institute of Technology and as a principal at The Monitor Group, a strategy and marketing consulting company. He also sits on the board of Multitude Bank. He has a PhD from the University of Texas, Austin.

FRÉDÉRIC DALSACE is a Professor of Marketing and Strategy at IMD, a position he has held since 2019. His research covers several areas, including strategic B2B issues such as customer centricity, outsourcing, buyer-seller relationship strategies, service-based business models, and value-based strategies. His work in this area has been published in journals such as *Strategic Management Journal, Harvard Business Review,* and *Business Horizons.* Frédéric co-created the Leading Customer-Centric Strategies open program at IMD, and he has been directing custom programs for firms like Valmet, Safran, Caterpillar, Traton, Porsche, Schneider Electric, and Holcim.

His interest in marketing strategies also led him to investigate managerial decision-making processes, and in particular the types of questions that managers ask before making decisions. His research on this topic appeared in *Harvard Business Review.*

In addition, Frédéric has been working on the topic of sustainability for almost twenty years. At HEC Paris, where he previously taught for sixteen years, he held the Social Business/Enterprise and Poverty Chair, working and publishing with co-chair and Nobel laureate Professor Muhammad Yunus. This research appeared in journals such as *Harvard Business Review, Journal of Social Business, Business Horizon*, and *Revue Française de Gestion.*

Since his arrival at IMD, Frédéric has continued to work on sustainability issues with Goutam Challagalla. They have published two articles in *Harvard Business Review,* one of which was selected for *HBR's 10 Must Reads 2025.* He has been teaching custom programs on sustainability for firms like Atlas Copco, Assa Abloy, Tetra Pak, Siemens, and Nestlé, as well as open programs such as Leading Sustainable Business Transformation and Advanced Management Program. Together with Goutam, he co-directs the Integrating Sustainability into Strategy open program, where *Clean Winners* concepts are taught and further elaborated upon.

Frédéric has been among the top fifty case writers in the world, and he is the author of more than twenty-five academic cases, for which he received several awards. He has also received numerous teaching awards, and in 2025 was named "Best Teacher" in the Master's in Sustainability and Technology program of the Enterprise 4 Society, which is co-managed by IMD, EPFL, and University of Lausanne.

Prior to his academic career, Frédéric had more than ten years of experience in the business world. He worked in the sales and marketing departments of several industrial companies such as Michelin and CarnaudMetalbox, both in Europe and in Japan. He was also a strategy consultant with McKinsey & Company for more than three years.

Frédéric is an alumnus of HEC Paris. He holds an MBA from Harvard Business School, and both an MSc and a PhD in Management from INSEAD.